New Directions for
Student Services

John H. Schuh
EDITOR-IN-CHIEF

Elizabeth J. Whitt
ASSOCIATE EDITOR

Technology in Student Affairs
Supporting Student Learning and Services

Kevin Kruger

EDITOR

Number 112 • Winter 2005
Jossey-Bass
San Francisco

TECHNOLOGY IN STUDENT AFFAIRS: SUPPORTING STUDENT LEARNING AND SERVICES
Kevin Kruger (ed.)
New Directions for Student Services, no. 112
John H. Schuh, Editor-in-Chief
Elizabeth J. Whitt, Associate Editor

NEW DIRECTIONS FOR STUDENT SERVICES (ISSN 0164-7970, e-ISSN 1536-0695) is part of The Jossey-Bass Higher and Adult Education Series and is published quarterly by Wiley Subscription Services, Inc., A Wiley Company, at Jossey-Bass, 989 Market Street, San Francisco, California 94103-1741. Periodicals Postage Paid at San Francisco, California, and at additional mailing offices. POSTMASTER: Send address changes to New Directions for Student Services, Jossey-Bass, 989 Market Street, San Francisco, California 94103-1741.

New Directions for Student Services is indexed in College Student Personnel Abstracts and Contents Pages in Education.

Microfilm copies of issues and articles are available in 16mm and 35mm, as well as microfiche in 105mm, through University Microfilms Inc., 300 North Zeeb Road, Ann Arbor, Michigan 48106-1346.

SUBSCRIPTIONS cost $75 for individuals and $180 for institutions, agencies, and libraries. See ordering information page at end of book.

EDITORIAL CORRESPONDENCE should be sent to the Editor-in-Chief, John H. Schuh, N 243 Lagomarcino Hall, Iowa State University, Ames, Iowa 50011.

www.josseybass.com

CONTENTS

EDITOR'S NOTES

I remember with great fondness my personal introduction to information technology as a sophomore in high school with the purchase of the Texas Instrument TI 3000, one of the first desktop calculators available on the retail market. It sold for $84.95. Since that first foray into technology, I recall purchasing the first "touch screen" HP desktops in the mid-1980s and managing the installation of a "token-ring" network for the admissions office in which I worked (both of which became obsolete soon after purchase). I recall multiple database programs written by burgeoning computer science student geniuses, whose programs often only partially satisfied the intended purpose and whose chronic lack of documentation meant a doomed future. Finally, I recall the high-tech rush of the early 1990s, when the for-profit sector "discovered" student affairs and rolled out scores of software solutions, from portal software to student health solutions to career exploration and placement programs. Many, if not most of these companies are no longer in business.

I started writing and paying attention to technology in student affairs back in the early 1980s, when student affairs was largely concerned with the use of productivity tools and how programs such as word processing would save offices from burning stencils and mimeographing flyers and large-scale mailings. The early to mid-1990s were spent focusing on how to begin using e-mail to serve our communication needs and how the rise of the Internet and Web pages would enable student affairs to communicate with students more effectively. The last ten years have seen technology become ubiquitous. It is part of virtually every task and project we undertake.

Where are we now? Technology innovation continues to advance. Technology has now become a central tool in creating 24/7 self-service experiences for students interacting with campus administrative functions. Recent technologies now create the real possibility of moving beyond administrative functions to playing a central role in student learning, community development, and student development.

Thankfully, we have evolved into increasingly sophisticated technology solutions that meet the needs of an increasingly diverse student body, many of whom may or may not ever reside on campus, or for that matter, ever sit in a traditional classroom.

While no one would argue about the key role technology plays on the modern college campus, resources, both fiscal and human, have limited the pace of technological innovation in student affairs. The most recent history of technology in higher education has focused on two movements, often to the exclusion of student affairs. The migration to large-enterprise student database management systems and the implementation of online courseware

(BlackBoard, WebCT, and so forth) in the classroom have committed signifi-cant information technology resources on campus. As a result, innovations in student affairs have often come slowly.

This volume attempts to capture the current thinking around the use of technology in student affairs. It is difficult to write about technology with-out the rapid advances in technology making the writing immediately out-dated. It would come as no surprise that since the last *New Directions for Student Services* issue on the topic, edited by Engstrom and Kruger in 1997 (no. 78: *Using Technology to Promote Student Learning: Opportunities for Today and Tomorrow*), many of the chapters there are significantly out-of-date and were so within three years of the publication. While the pace of technology change continues to be fast, this issue focuses less on the technology and more on the ways in which the technology is altering the organization of stu-dent affairs, the ways in which the lines between campus-based students and distance learners are blurring, and the increasing role technology is playing in student learning.

In Chapter One, Larry Moneta, who also authored the first chapter of the 1997 issue, discusses a range of issues related to managing information technology and provides a framework for the ways in which technology has changed the business practices of student affairs. In Chapter Two, Pat Shea reviews the work of the Learning Anytime Anywhere Project (LAAP) funded by the Fund for the Improvement of Postsecondary Education (FIPSE) to create Web-based services for online student learners. In Chapter Three, Nessa Kleinglass discusses the need for student affairs to play a more central role in technology conversations on campus and reviews her research on the technology competencies necessary for student affairs professionals. In Chap-ter Four, Leslie A. Dare, Lisa P. Zapata, and Amanda G. Thomas review research results on the needs of distance learners and their use of Web-based and campus-based student services. Janet Kendell, in Chapter Five, describes the "Web of Student Services" and outlines specific technologies that repre-sent the evolution of online student services for both on-campus and dis-tance learners. In Chapter Six, Marilee J. Bresciani examines the roles of electronic co-curricular portfolios in providing assessment data on the stu-dent learning experience of students. Maria Tess Shier, in Chapter Seven, looks at a series of key issues that emerging technology has created, from file-sharing to opportunities to build virtual communities. In Chapter Eight, Gary L. Kleemann outlines the evolution of generations of Web sites that have progressed from simple information dissemination to relationship build-ing. In Chapter Nine, I provide final thoughts on key issues to be considered in planning for the impact of technology in student affairs.

Kevin Kruger
Editor

KEVIN KRUGER is associate executive director of the National Association of Stu-dent Personnel Administrators (NASPA).

1

The author addresses two critical questions related to technology: How has students' use of technology influenced student affairs work? How do we best align our business practices with advances in information technology?

Technology and Student Affairs: Redux

Larry Moneta

That technology has and continues to influence the work of student affairs is certainly quite obvious. In fact, it is difficult to conceive of any student affairs practice operating without some technological applications, from hand-held devices to Web-based processes. The information technology director has become a critical position on the student affairs leadership team and e-mail communication is both ubiquitous and overwhelming. In short, the educational and administrative functions of student affairs are fully intertwined with various technologies, with some consequences consistent with previous forecasts (Moneta, 1997).

With technology so pervasive throughout our work, what are the unanswered questions worthy of consideration? They include the following:

- How have changes in students' uses of technology and in their expectations about technologies influenced the work of student affairs?
- What business practices are we engaged in as student affairs practitioners and how best do we align technologies with them?
- What competencies are essential for student affairs practitioners in order to apply technological tools most effectively so as to optimize educational and administrative efforts?
- What are the resource implications (financial and human) associated with technology and student affairs?
- What differentiates the various student affairs departments and what distinctive technological applications are influencing their work?

New Directions for Student Services, no. 112, Winter 2005 © Wiley Periodicals, Inc.

Student Differences

The use of computers by college students is nearly universal, with 85.7 percent reporting using a personal computer on a frequent basis, compared to 27.3 percent in 1985 (Higher Education Research Institute [HERI]), Fall 2004). Though gender differences have diminished, overall differences across racial or ethnic groups have increased. Though minimal differences are noted among students from high-income families, differences are sharp across racial or ethnic groups at lower income levels (HERI, 2004). The Pew Foundation's Internet and American Life Project (Rainie and Horrigan, 2005) offers additional evidence of the comprehensive reliance by adult Americans on computers and the Web for a variety of information relevant to daily life. Data provided by the Student Monitor's Spring 2005 Lifestyle & Media study demonstrate the overwhelming dependency students have on cell phones, entertainment devices (including music and television), and transactional technologies, including credit cards.

Thus, one might imagine a typical day in the life of a college student beginning with a wake-up device, followed by a hand-held, vibrating dental hygiene instrument, all as prelude to a first bout with overnight (or late morning) e-mail correspondence. Concurrent Instant Messaging, Web review of the news, sports, and weather, and a calendar sync with a PDA might very well follow. With a remote-control unit in hand and a couple of buttons pressed, live or prerecorded television shows can be scanned—preferably with the convenience of a digital video recorder. A series of cell phone calls ensues to establish meal plans, meeting logistics, and parental contact (for the first of several occasions yet to follow that day). Academic obligations follow, and with a check of Blackboard, our young student is now up-to-date with course expectations and assignments.

Time remains for some fun, and our student grapples with whether to spend it with a new video game or search for social contacts on the Facebook (www.thefacebook.com). Our multitasking expert decides to do both! As time approaches for class, new music is loaded on an MP3 player (most likely the kind with white earphones) and the laptop is stuffed into an already burgeoning book bag, along with this panoply of technological devices, and the day begins.

Much more could be added to this fable: time spent blogging, digital photography by a dedicated camera or, more likely, by camera phone, and further e-mail communication by Blackberry or a similar device. With campuswide wireless broadband, these activities can continue all over campus: in classrooms, dining halls, lounges, and under the shade of the campus oak or palm tree.

With burgeoning access to multiple technology devices and unparalleled data access, what are the implications for student development—for the individual and community? Is there a relationship between this proliferation of isolated modes of communication and entertainment and the growing mental health crisis we face? Are the burgeoning challenges of cheating and related ethical offenses derived in any way from our technological revolution? These are complex questions and issues requiring further research and analysis.

There are, however, more immediate consequences to a life of gadgets and keyboards. As noted in 1997 (Moneta, 1997) and even more evident today, we serve a student body that is used to around-the-clock access to services and students who are remarkably awake and electronically active throughout the night. Their ability to multitask is finely honed and undoubtedly fuels attention deficits and related disorders.

This proliferation of technology has many positive attributes. Student social networks transcend geographical (and time zone) boundaries, and relationships are sustained across generations, institutions, and interest areas. Social networks evolve into professional networks that support career development and job attainment. Alumni connections with their institutions are sustained through electronic communications, and institutional loyalty is ultimately enhanced. The work of student affairs is benefited by these relationships, as students find support from peers and elders and sustain friendships and mentor relationships well beyond their collegiate experiences.

As will be noted in detail later in this chapter, campus practices and, in particular, student affairs practices are often ill suited to accommodate the technologically proficient college student. Love and Estanek (2004) offer thoughtful consideration of the value of technology and caution us to deploy technology carefully to optimize our work. Too often, they note, the demands of technology hinder the effectiveness of our efforts by drawing away time, money, and energy that could be more effectively used on behalf of student needs.

Technological Competencies and Business Practices

In light of such dramatic change in the technological prowess and engagement by students, what should we expect of student affairs staff? One might immediately assume the need for dramatic remediation of technological competency among current staff as well as the expectation of technological expertise at or above the level of entering students for new employees. While these might be reasonable expectations if one presumes the need for staff to compete with students' technological skills, in reality, tackling this learning curve may not be the most effective use of staff time. In fact, with the proliferation of technological applications and devices abounding, the most critical competency requirement for staff will be mastering the skills necessary to analyze student affairs needs and work processes along with increased education to understand better how students perceive and use technology.

The operations of student affairs cover a spectrum of activities encompassing formal administrative processes, such as appointment scheduling, room assignments, and space reservations as well as our qualitative work as advisors to clubs and organizations, limit-setters in various behavioral circumstances, and educators through one-to-one consultations and presenting programs. We accomplish all of this and more through administratively segmented structures called divisions and departments, particularly at the larger institutions, but equally evident even at the smaller schools. Our enterprises employ large staffs, have significant revenues and expenses, and are subject to formal and often complex evaluation and assessment models—all processes that can be significantly enhanced by critically analyzing and revamping business processes and the appropriate application of technology tools.

Beede and Burnett (1999) provide compelling arguments for analyzing business processes in student services. Albeit with a focus on more purely administrative functions, such as enrollment management and registration processes, they encourage student service practitioners to understand the work flow that supports the transactional relationships between students and the institution. Automation, then, becomes a tool by which those transactions are simplified and optimized and the relationship with the student enhanced. These same principles apply to the human service components of student affairs, such as counseling, leadership development, and residence-hall community building. With each, a transactional relationship is developed between students (or student groups) and student affairs staff. The human transaction may involve counseling, advising, mentoring, or formal teaching, but the engagement is, nonetheless, a transaction of some service delivery or information dissemination that can be enhanced by thoughtful consideration of the components of each transaction and the application of technology where appropriate and effective.

An essential competency, then, for every student affairs practitioner is the capacity to examine and analyze the nature of the relationships with our various clients: students first and foremost, but also parents, alumni, faculty, and staff. Competence as process analyst will enable student affairs employees at all levels to uncover practices that disadvantage or optimize the provision of services to students and others. Only then can the application of technology be an effective component of student affairs operations.

Having minimized the technological competence necessary for individual student affairs practitioners, we would now emphasize the critical need for technological expertise within student affairs organizations as well as in partnership with institutional information technology organizations. Due to rapid and continuous change within the technological landscape, it has become much more important that the student affairs team now include individuals knowledgeable about technological solutions to process challenges uncovered through workflow analysis. Examples of such recent process-based innovations include the use of PDAs by residence hall staff to record residence hall room inspections then upload the information to a central database; flexible content-management systems to localize content with functional users rather than technical support personnel to ensure timely delivery of Web-based information. Moreover, hand-held computers coupled with Bluetooth-equipped cell phones, may solve the remote communications needs, and a searchable database may address the desire to track community service initiatives. The key is to first identify the support need and then, with the expertise offered by technology specialists, to identify and adopt the technological application that best suits the circumstances. To do so requires access to up-to-date technological competencies, either as a direct member of the student affairs staff or as a reliable partnered, contracted, or purchased service.

Applications for student affairs use also are becoming more integrated and more complicated. Many enterprise applications that serve institutional need (such as student record systems, financial and human resource management systems, and applications that support fundraising activities) now include modules applicable to student affairs needs. For example, institution-wide student record applications can also track and record student involvement in various clubs and activities and may include modules for career portfolio design for individual student use. Systemwide applications offer space-management components, room reservation options, and other facility-related applications viable for student affairs use. Even smaller packages designed for more localized uses offer generalizable utility, such as a housing assignment applications suite that can also serve visitor and conferencing uses.

These very expensive and extremely complicated applications further reinforce the need for access to technological expertise within a planning model that assumes careful consideration of the business processes to be advanced and improved. From the perspective of the senior student affairs officer, the opportunities for enhancing student service and support are substantial, but the consequences of making the wrong choices are even more daunting and potentially disastrous. One is more likely to make the wrong call if attracted to a technological application in advance of really understanding the business need to be developed or enhanced.

The Costs and Opportunities of Technology

Creative collaboration among institutions and commercial vendors has resulted in the development of viable campus software solutions that were largely unimagined even a few years ago. As predicted by Katz (1996), colleges and universities have partnered with nontraditional vendors to create new markets and products in the higher-education market. Applying work-process and change-management principles drawn from the corporate sector to student service and educational processes has been difficult, but has also resulted in innovative and creative changes to decades-old, less than student-friendly practices. The advent of these new systems has made it relatively easy for administrators to obtain immediate, accurate, real-time information about students. Students themselves update addresses, register for classes, add points to meal plans, apply for financial aid, pay bursar bills, order books, and access course information on a 24/7 basis.

Economic Implications. Though delivering nearly all that futurists envisioned, these systems came to most campuses at a different price than most anticipated. The complexity of developing common data definitions and standardized business processes across functional areas long used to relative data- and work-process isolation requires a level of sustained effort generally underpredicted and often under-resourced by institutions. The higher-education landscape is littered with stories of implementations gone bad because technology was viewed as a solution without rethinking essential business processes. In their compendium of best practices for the twenty-first century, Beede and Burnett (1999) advise that identifying and understanding customer needs, rethinking business processes, and planning for organizational change are the essential ingredients for using technology as a change agent.

Partnerships with commercial consultants and vendors, while bringing a level of expertise and experience to the project not available on campus, can also result in the clash of corporate and academic cultures over decision making and resources. In the early days of the re-engineering blitz on college campuses, administrators naively predicted great cost savings while anticipating the achievement of widespread access to better and more reliable data. Generally, the latter objective was achieved, but seldom with significant overall savings to the institution. Often underanticipated were the ongoing costs of these new institutional systems, which require powerful server hardware and maintenance by highly skilled IT professionals. Since systems are mission-critical, they must be backed up regularly and are usually redundant, either with mirrored sites or swappable parts, in case of hardware failure. These services represent new costs in addition to licensing fees for both application and database software. Dedicated technical staff effort is necessary to maintain, upgrade, and monitor the systems. Some institutions sought to temper additional infrastructure costs through innovative outsourcing planning and implementation partnerships with external vendors (VanHorn-Grassmeyer and Stoner, 2001).

Personnel costs increased, as frequent functional users generally must have a level of technical skill unnecessary in the days of mainframe legacy or departmental PC database systems. Ensuring these new staff competencies means additional and, often, continuously updated training. In some cases, the competency gaps were too big, necessitating reorganizations and replacement of lower-level employees with more highly skilled and thus highly paid staffs. Some institutions also found it necessary to create entirely new departments of expert technical and functional users to support their institutional applications. The necessity and consequent additional cost of developing simple Web-based interfaces for use by casual administrative users and students quickly became important to many institutions, resulting in additional cost and effort.

In today's world, most student service organizations have managed to get a computer on the desktop of every employee. Some have even managed to develop funding strategies to upgrade and replace equipment and software. As more institutional systems have been rolled out, the need for faster and more powerful computers increased. Few organizations anticipated how quickly four- and five-year replacement cycles for desktop computers would dwindle to two- and three-year rotations. Nor did they anticipate how changing service-delivery processes would increase demand for portable devices. Though hardware costs have dropped dramatically in the past few years, the advent of roving staff to support service-center models, programmatic philosophies focusing more on outreach to students "where they live," and increased telecommuting have resulted in increased demand for laptops, PDAs, cell phones and other devices. The proliferation of portable devices adds cost both in hardware and support, as employees often now have multiple devices, all of which need to be synchronous with and able to access institutional systems. As more colleges and universities have embraced the 24/7 service model expected by students and families, Web-enabled applications, e-mail, and other technology tools must be available continuously, with downtime for hardware maintenance increasingly difficult to find. Working from multiple offices as well as at home due to the rise of flexible scheduling coupled with the expectation of expanded availability to student "customers," employees may now reasonably expect that the cost of cell phone plans and cable or DSL home service be covered by their institutions.

As enterprise systems for student services become ubiquitous, institutional tolerance for redundant, shadow, and separate systems has been reduced. However, since no enterprise system does everything well, new challenges face student service organizations in selecting and integrating important subsidiary systems with the enterprise systems. These systems include a spectrum of student services support systems, such as identity-card management, venue scheduling and event registration, housing assignments, incident reporting, career services, dining, and appointment scheduling. The ease with which student data can be extracted from institutional systems comes with additional risk-management challenges relevant to the Family Educational Rights and Privacy Act (FERPA) and the Health Insurance Portability Accountability Act of 1996 (HIPAA) regulations. While data extracts from mainframe systems required the expertise and intervention of a technical professional knowledgeable in the appropriate handling of the data, it is now often relatively simple for staff to extract these data themselves and import it into FileMaker, Access, or similar, homegrown, databases.

Though enterprise systems have brought increases in accuracy, efficiency, and customer service, student service organizations face many new or increased costs related to the general implementation of technology tools and systems. Facing increased scrutiny by governing bodies, boards, and the public, cuts in programs and personnel are easy targets as organizations struggle to balance technology achievements with the traditional personal touch so valued by student affairs professionals.

Organizational and Staffing Impacts. The age of popular access to the Internet dawned only in 1994 with the release by Netscape of its free Web browser, Mosaic. With 63 percent of the over-eighteen population in the United States now going online (Rainie and Horrigan, 2005), students and their families are used to accessing the Internet every day. Students access the Internet to answer virtually every information need: news, comparison shopping, vacation and business travel planning, romance, access to music and the arts, online auctions, purchasing stocks and bonds, and getting information on virtually any topic, individual, or subject. The expectation that information and services will be available according to the 24/7 service demands and Web savvy of today's students has resulted in efforts by colleges and universities to transition many routine and relatively simple institutional transactions to the Web. As more transactions are handled directly by students, the need for relatively low-skilled workers handling paper and data entry or reception has diminished. The advent of student service centers has created more need for better-educated, skilled, and technologically savvy front-office personnel. Often, fewer positions are needed once services are consolidated. Some institutions have been able to make workforce adjustments gradually by not filling vacancies and retraining existing employees. However, because new jobs require skills and knowledge that are greater in scope and depth than the old jobs, workforce savings are generally not achieved with staff reductions.

The explosion of Web-based information presents new challenges for staff used to information dissemination via print or other traditional means. Student affairs professionals must master and keep up-to-date with technical skills relevant to their roles and responsibilities, be knowledgeable of vended products and technology solutions applicable to their work, and balance this technical competency on a solid conceptual foundation of knowledge about students (Blimling and Whitt, 1999). Technical competencies for new staff now include proficiencies in office productivity tools, database creation and management, and management of Web-site content in addition to strategic planning, communications, and work-process analysis skills. With increased access to data protected by FERPA, HIPAA, and other institutional, state, and federal regulations, ongoing education and training efforts are required to keep staff up-to-date with relevant policies.

Many student service organizations increasingly are large enough and technologically mature enough to warrant and require dedicated IT staff created within the group or via assignment from a central IT organization. What was more common in organizations such as residence life and housing, admissions, and registrar in terms of IT staffing and support has become common for entire organizations, with many creating their own IT departments. Creating new funding sources or diverting existing sources to support these new staffing needs is challenging, but essential.

Anticipating Student Demand. Word about a technology solution that is innovative and successful at one institution spreads rapidly among students across the country, virtually ensuring clamoring and similar demand at other institutions (Ardaiolo, Bender, and Roberts, 2005). Witness the plethora of student portals, online career services, and Web-based instructional and course-delivery systems that have emerged in recent years. Today's college students have grown up with computers. Unlike older generations, they assume technology is a part of daily life. Their expectations of access on campus to technologies similar to those they are used to in daily life will be high, and their patience with the pace of technology change in higher education will be low. Students may well ask why they can't reserve a meeting room online when they can go to any hotel chain in the country and reserve a guest room. Wireless access is becoming common in city centers, so why not everywhere on campus? Hotel guests can download information on dining and entertainment options in their location to their PDAs or WAP phones, so students may expect similar information to be downloadable when they enter the campus student center. As online appointment systems become more common in the health care and private industry sectors, students will expect to make their campus advising, counseling, and health care appointments in the same way.

With their necessary partnerships in the corporate world, career centers have been among the most innovative among student service areas in the use of technology to deliver services to students. With a plethora of career-planning and job-placement information available on the Internet, most career centers have developed dynamic Web sites of their own or partnered with external vendors, such as monster.com and experience.com, to create mini student portals. Career center staffs have studied the impact of technology in their profession carefully by examining the appropriateness of Web-delivered services, considering how student needs can be met with technology tools, and determining whether technology-enhanced services adhere to the ethical principles established by their professional association (Davidson, 2001). The development of the customizable career center student portal offered by several vendors enables a college or university career center to brand its own site while offering access to thousands of Internet job postings. Customizable and individual e-mail communications, pop-up messages, and outreach tools enable the career center to reach large numbers of students while maintaining the semblance of personalized service to individual students. Sophisticated reporting tools manage data in ways that allow career center staff to constantly and efficiently monitor the student, employer, and alumni career-related activities and further manage and customize messages, outreach, and services. The integration of these career systems with institutional alumni databases affords another mechanism to maintain and foster long-term relationships with graduates through the ongoing provision of career services and opportunities for mentoring.

Campus residence-life and housing departments also have taken advantage of technology solutions designed to address student needs and simplify often complicated assignment and check-in–check-out processes. Web-based interfaces allow students 24/7 access to submit an application for housing, select their rooms, specify roommate choice, view and make payments on their accounts, and request maintenance. Database solutions enable housing staff to manage large inventories of residence hall rooms and apartments, including tracking maintenance and housekeeping. Assigning and changing rooms, changing rates, and billing have become largely automated tasks. Partnerships between institutions and vendors of major student information and housing systems ensure the easy exchange of student data, thus ensuring faster and virtually error-free transactions, as well as increasing data reliability and accuracy. Again, the ability to create customized and personalized letters and e-mails to students is standard in these systems. Interesting new features include wireless tools (usually PDAs) that enable staff to manage housing processes such as check in and checkout, inventory, and even incident reporting from any location on campus. These innovations mean that staff can meet and check in a busload of summer campers or conference attendees on-site, submit damage reports and schedule housekeeping while walking through the building, and access accurate student information to create an incident or judicial report at the scene.

Student health centers have drawn on appointment scheduling and medical information system concepts born in the greater health care field to customize similar services for their college and university clientele. Comprehensive medical information is common on student health center Web sites, enabling students to access a variety of health-related information at any time of the day or night. Newer innovations include Web-based triage systems, such as the "24/7 WebMed" site at the University of Central Florida, in which students are guided through a series of questions about symptoms, resulting in action recommendations for next steps, including options for self-treatment, scheduling an appointment, or advice to seek immediate medical attention. Other student health centers, such as those at Brigham Young University, Georgetown University, and University of California, San Diego have developed their own or partnered with vendors to create online offices through which students can handle a variety of health-related concerns, such as sending secure messages to providers, reviewing their own health records, and making appointments online. College counseling centers have adopted technology tools that appeal to their student clientele, including self-paced, online orientation modules addressing the adjustment concerns of new students, online self-screening, and "ask a counselor" services.

In touch with new students, admissions offices and orientation programs at colleges and universities are among the leaders in using technology. Self-paced, online campus tours are common, often offering the user a choice of student tour guide. To engage and retain the attention of prospective students, these online tours often include a variety of media, such as video and audio clips with key administrators, faculty, and students; inside views of campus buildings; and interactive maps. Online orientation tutorials guide new students and their parents through the adjustment and transition issues encountered by new students, while they also provide more up-to-date information about courses, programs, and services than can be communicated through printed publications.

Conclusion

Student affairs is a profession comprised of diverse and distinctive practices intended to enhance the educational experience of students. Practices include formal administrative structures as well as direct human service support through counseling, advising, and various mentorship roles. In all cases, staffs interact with students as well as with faculty, parents, alumni, and many others in various transactional relationships involving processes ranging from the simple to the complex. These transactional relationships constitute the business processes of our profession. The quality of our services to students and others is directly associated with the efficiency and effectiveness of our business process transactions, and increasingly, these processes have become automated through a plethora of technological applications designed for student affairs practices.

Concurrently, students' use of technologies and students' experiences and expectations have evolved rapidly. Students expect around-the-clock access to information and support, and they are increasingly facile with and dependent on a host of technological devices. Thus, student affairs practitioners are further pressed to deploy technological tools to meet student demands, but are ill equipped to identify optimal applications to meet those needs. To become more proficient users of technology will require that student affairs staff be more competent in analyzing and understanding the business processes associated with our various practices (health, housing, student activities, career services, and so on) and in identifying appropriate technological applications that are best suited to improving the transactions associated with each of those practices. The latter skill set will also require that student affairs organizations have access to skilled IT professionals, either as employees of the student affairs unit, through partnerships with institutional IT staff, or through contracted service agreements.

Technology is seductive. On any given day, one can expect to encounter yet another novel application, Web site, or device. The pressure to succumb to the latest and greatest technology can be overwhelming—and expensive! It is ever more critical that student affairs staffs focus on the outcomes intended by our various services and let technology follow—not lead—a thoughtful consideration of the roles and relationships associated with our profession.

References

Ardaiolo, F. P., Bender, B. E., and Roberts, G. "Campus Services: What Do Students Expect?" In T. E. Miller, B. E. Bender, and J. H. Schuh (eds.), *Promoting Reasonable Expectations*. San Francisco: Jossey-Bass, 2005.

Beede, M., and Burnett, D. (eds.). *Planning for Student Services: Best Practices for the 21st Century*. Ann Arbor: Society for College and University Planning, 1999.

Blimling, G. S., and Whitt, E. J. *Good Practice in Student Affairs: Principles to Foster Student Learning*. San Francisco: Jossey-Bass, 1999.

Davidson, M. "The Computerization of Career Services: Critical Issues to Consider." *Journal of Career Development*, 2001, 27(3), 217–228.

Higher Education Research Institute (HERI). *The American Freshman: National Norms for Fall 2004*. Los Angeles: University of California, Los Angeles, 2005.

Katz, R. "Technology-Enriched Teaching and Learning: A Business Planning Perspective." In Coopers and Lybrand, LLP, S. Johnson, and S. Rush (eds.). *Reinventing the University: Managing and Financing Institutions of Higher Education*. New York: Wiley, 1996.

Love, P., and Estanek, S. *Rethinking Student Affairs Practice*. San Francisco: Jossey-Bass, 2004.

Moneta, L. "The Integration of Technology with the Management of Student Services." In C. McHugh Engstrom and K. W. Kruger, (eds.), *Using Technology to Promote Student Learning*. New Directions for Student Services, no. 78. San Francisco: Jossey-Bass, 1997.

Rainie, L., and Horrigan, J. "The Mainstreaming of Online Life." Pew Internet & American Life Project, 1/25/2005. http://www.pewinternet.org/PPF/r/148/report_display.asp. Accessed April 15, 2005.

Student Monitor. *Lifestyle & Media Study*. Spring, 2005. Ridgewood, N.J.: Student Monitor. (Information available at http://www.studentmonitor. com)

VanHorn-Grassmeyer, K., and Stoner, K. "Adventures in Outsourcing." In L. H. Dietz and E. J. Enchelmayer (eds.), Developing External Partnerships for Cost-Effective, Enhanced Service. New Directions for Student Services, no. 96. San Francisco: Jossey-Bass, 2001.

Western Cooperative for Educational Telecommunications (WCET). *Annual Report—2001*. Boulder, Colo.: WCET, 2002.

LARRY MONETA is vice president for student affairs and adjunct associate professor of public policy studies, Hart Leadership Program, at Duke University.

2

*Student services Web sites need to be student-centered,
convenient, and efficient in order to address the complex
needs of both distance and campus-based students.*

Serving Students Online: Enhancing Their Learning Experience

Patricia A. Shea

Putting student services online is no longer optional for colleges and universities. Postsecondary students expect to interact with their institutions over the Web, and they judge their schools in part by the type of experience they have. If that experience is convenient, efficient, and student-centered, they have a positive reaction. If it provides a virtual runaround and inaccurate or outdated information, they have a negative one.

Today, an institution's Web site often provides the first impression a student has with a campus. Carefully designed services like those at Weber State University in Utah (www.weber.edu) use that opportunity to begin to build a relationship with a prospective student. There, the student has the option of providing a little contact information and expressing some areas of interest, while university staff use specialized software to evaluate the interest level of the student and return any communications. The next day the student gets an e-mail with links to a personalized Weber State home page created for him or her, with links to areas of interest noted in their initial communication and related links that might be of further interest. A photo and e-mail address identify a student ambassador who is available to answer questions or provide more information. The message is this: We care about you and your interest in our school!

Contrast this experience with that of students who visit the home page of another campus and are greeted with institution-centric language that focuses on the school's internal structure. The content appears to be replicated from the school catalog, and there is no attempt to speak directly to

NEW DIRECTIONS FOR STUDENT SERVICES, no. 112, Winter 2005 © Wiley Periodicals, Inc.

them. They are on their own to find the information they seek. There is no path for a prospective student. Rather, he or she must click around for information about majors in various departments, read long lists of fees associated with various tuition levels, and download a PDF of the admissions application if they want more information. The message: If you come to school here, you are on your own! How an institution puts its services online is very important.

Student Services Available Online

From the point of view of a distance student—especially one who cannot come to campus—the answer to the question of whether all student services should be available online is yes. Certainly, as campuses put more courses and programs online, they need to be sure that they are providing the same level of access to services for both their on-campus and their distance students. And today, even campus-based students prefer the convenience of online services.

Which services are these? And, even more basically, what are student services? In the recent Learning Anytime Anywhere Partnership (LAAP) project funded by the U.S. Department of Education and its Fund for the Improvement of Postsecondary Education (FIPSE), "Beyond the Administrative Core: Creating Web-Based Student Services for Online Learners," WCET (Western Cooperative for Educational Telecommunications, 2003) worked with three institutional partners and one corporate partner: Kansas State University, Kapi'olani Community College, Regis University, and SCT (now known as SunGard-SCT), a manufacturer of student information systems. Each partner had a different understanding of and definition for student services. In order to collaborate on the design of new Web services, the partners had to come to some consensus. The diagram in Figure 2.1 reflects the consensus of the project's partners. It may not fit all campuses, but it provides a frame of reference from which to proceed.

In the LAAP project, the services were divided into five suites: administrative core plus academic, communications, personal services, and student communities suites. Each suite contains a collection of services the partners agreed should be available to online learners. Note that the outer edge of the web has dotted lines to show that this is not an all-inclusive list, but rather an evolving one. At the center of the web is the notation "one student and a curriculum," a reminder to design personalized and customized services from the student's point of view—something the web architecture makes possible and today's students expect.

This web of services was useful throughout the LAAP project in helping to build consensus on the partner campuses about the scope of services that should be available to all students. It has been very useful in other WCET projects, too, especially the development of the Audit Tool to be discussed later in this chapter.

Figure 2.1. Student Services for Online Learners

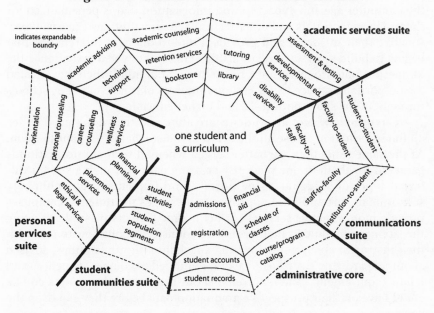

Best Practices in Student Services Online

Although providing student services online is in its infancy, there are some characteristics that current best practices indicate are important for what services should be.

Student-Centered. Services should be redesigned from the students' point of view, using language that is familiar to them, rather than the internal language of the institution. The new best practices have a customer-service focus. At Mesa Community College in Arizona, information about financial aid, which can be so confusing to students, is simplified into an easy, step-by-step process, with language that speaks directly to the student.

Blended. Historically, services were added on most campuses as the need for them arose. There was no holistic plan, and each service operated with a high degree of autonomy—many with their own student data system, policies, and procedures. Using some of today's technologies, it is possible to integrate some of these systems and services, even as they remain separated in the physical environment. These new blended services, such as enrollment services—an integration of admissions, registration, financial aid, and student accounts—can be more effective and efficient for both the student and the institution. For example, at Arizona State University a student can create and save her four-year plan, identifying course sequences. This plan can be used to interact seamlessly with her degree audit, search the catalog and schedule of classes, create a new schedule of classes, and register for those classes.

Personalized. Today's traditionally aged students have grown up in the computer age and expect to find information that is personalized for them. Through portals and other technologies, institutions can easily personalize their messages and provide a one-to-one text interchange that begins to build a personal relationship. This is the type of experience the Minnesota State Colleges and Universities had in mind when they created their e-portfolio service (www.efoliominnesota.com) now in use by schools throughout the state (both K–12 and higher education).

Customized. Not all students are alike and they don't need to see all the information or use all the services—just what is relevant to them. At the same time, they are better served when all related information is gathered for them in one place. By creating paths through a site for different types of students, using portals, and implementing technology solutions to sort and send appropriate messages to students, campuses provide more effective services. At Penn State University, students using the late-drop module in their portal are counseled about how to talk with their instructor about difficulties and check into tutoring options, advised about jeopardizing their financial aid, reminded of courses sequences and major requirements, and counseled about the impact dropping a course could have on their prospective graduation date before they can drop the course.

Customizable. Web-generation and other technology-savvy students prefer sites where they can change the views and add their personal links and other information. On the career services site at the University of Arizona (www.career.arizona.edu/index.aspx), students can store their personal links for the center in the left navigation bar, saving them time on future visits.

Convenient. More students are part time than full time today. Many work during the day and need access to services outside the traditional eight-to-five business day. Web services—not just information—available for extended hours (and, where possible, 24/7) better meet the needs of today's students. At the University of North Carolina at Greensboro, students can chat online with counselors during evenings and weekends. In addition, the staff at the virtual-information station can work from home and access a student's financial aid records via VPN connections to provide more specific advice.

Just-in-Time. In this media-rich world, many students suffer from information overload and sometimes overlook or ignore important messages or information. Services that take advantage of technology to track students and anticipate their needs by sending them appropriate information just before they need it help to ensure that their students stay engaged. At Regis University in Colorado, for example, automated triggers in the student information system keep track of a student's admissions progress and send personalized messages or reminders to keep the student on track.

Characteristics of Best Practices

Best-practice services also have other features, some of which are listed in this section.

Two-Way Communication Strategies. By using communication strategies that enhance a two-way exchange of information in real time, Web services come alive for students and provide more efficient service. Institutions that use status replies to submitted forms, chat rooms, knowledge-base agents, and pathways designed with artificial intelligence may provide a higher level of service than they could reasonably provide in a face-to-face environment. For example, when a student is browsing the Western Governors University (WGU) site for a few minutes, a pop-up window appears with live chat capability. A WGU representative pictured in the window introduces himself and asks if the student needs help.

Integrated Formats. This is truly the era of choice, and students want to select the ways in which they interact with the institution—face-to-face, or via the Web, e-mail, telephone, or print. Moreover, they expect the information and the services to be integrated in these different formats, so they are accessing one service available via different delivery methodologies—not several different versions (some more complete than others) of a single service. At the University of Minnesota Twin Cities, Web, in-person, and phone services are integrated via its ONE Stop for students, faculty or staff (http://onestop.umn.edu/onestop/).

Performance Indicators. Best practice services provide performance statements on their Web site that let students know what to expect and what to do if that expectation is not met. For example, if students are encouraged to ask questions related to a service via an e-mail link, they should also find a statement about when they can expect a reply and whom to contact if that expectation is not met. By providing suggestion boxes, mini opinion polls, grievance forms, and ombudsman contacts on the site, services can track student satisfaction and make constant improvements to serve their students better, increasing the likelihood of student success and retention. On Athabasca University's site, where there are "Expect the Best" standards (http://www.athabascau.ca/misc/expect), a student is advised about the length of time necessary for processing an application for admissions, evaluating a transcript, and responding to e-mail and other types of interactions. The university also supplies contact information for requesting assistance if these deadlines are not met.

Assessing an Institution's Student Services Online with the Audit Tool

The Audit Tool, developed by the author and Darlene Burnett in partnership with the Minnesota State Colleges and Universities (MnSCU), provides a way to measure the comprehensiveness and quality of an institution's online student services. The tool, designed from the student's point of view, currently focuses on twenty service areas, with others slated for development. The following services are contained in the audit tool: academic advising, admissions, assessment and testing, bookstore, career planning, catalog, communications (institution to student), financial aid, library, orientation, registration, personal counseling, placement services, schedule of classes, services for international students, services for students with disabilities, student accounts, student activities, technical support, and tutoring.

For each service, the tool contains a list of critical components, identified by experts in the field, that should be available to a student whether the service is available online or face-to-face. For example, some of the critical components of academic advising include making an appointment with an academic adviser, declaring a major, dropping a class, checking grades, and running a degree audit.

The tool contains descriptions for each of these critical components at four increasing levels of sophistication, based on an expansion of Burnett's description of four generations of online services (Burnett, 2002). Moving from one level to the next represents increased technology support, enabling reengineered services to deliver more customized and personalized service to the student.

As an example, let's take one of the critical components of academic advising, one captured in the phrase, "As a student, I can make an appointment with an academic adviser." Depending on the institution, a student is likely to have one of the following experiences online:

- *Generation Zero.* Student can find no information about making an appointment with an academic adviser.
- *Generation One.* Student can find office location and telephone number for scheduling an appointment.
- *Generation Two.* Student can click on adviser's e-mail address to launch a message to request an appointment.
- *Generation Three.* Student can view adviser's calendar online and schedule an appointment for one of the available times.
- *Generation Four.* Student can use his calendar and reason for the meeting as a filter against his adviser's calendar to find a selection of convenient appointment openings; he can select and schedule the appointment, along with a request for a reminder to be sent twenty-four hours in advance with appropriate preparation material.

Using the Audit Tool to identify current levels of service provided by an institution presents a way to set benchmarks. It also provides a way to build awareness among the institution's staff about higher levels of service and can supply a basis for developing a strategic plan for both short-term and long-term improvements.

Recently, access to the Audit Tool has be expanded to institutions on a contract basis through the Center for Transforming Student Services. Institutions may choose from two levels of service: they may use it with their staff as an online self-assessment instrument, or they may have the center use it to conduct an objective assessment, along with a more in-depth review of their Web services. The center, founded by WCET, MnSCU, and Seward, Inc., will have many other resources for institutions interested in transforming their student services, including examples of best practices, related articles, and professional development opportunities.

Overall Findings from Early Use of the Audit Tool

Researching the development of the Audit Tool and helping institutions understand how to put services online offer some overall findings and lessons learned:

Putting services online is still a work in progress for institutions. Although some schools have made great advancements in this area, many still have a few critical components missing in each of their services. As schools put services online, they generally progress from Generation One to Generation Two rather quickly. Generation Three services are more complex, requiring integration with the student information system and a secure interface(s) or portal. Since these services require a larger allocation of staff time and funding, schools are much slower to put these online. Generation Four services are even scarcer, and it does not appear that any school is yet at Generation Four across the board. Indeed, it may be several years before this happens, given the significance of the changes in policies, procedures, and staffing that commonly must occur to put such services in place.

The staff and leadership may not know what is on their site. It is surprising how often an institution's staff and leadership really do not know what is on their site. Sometimes staff assumes that information they consider common knowledge is readily apparent, only to find that it is never mentioned on the site. In other cases, a student service department may change a policy or staffing, yet weeks may pass before the new information is available to students on the Web. More commonly, several different departments may each be putting the same information up in their section of the Web site. Not only is this an inefficient use of staff time, the content is often inconsistent and confusing for students.

Best practices result from a vision plan. Those campuses that have taken the time to redesign their services from the student's perspective by working with cross-functional teams are more likely to exhibit best practices. This activity is more common at institutions where Web services are a high priority of the key executives. The leadership recognizes student services online as a way to provide more efficient and effective service and include their development in the strategic plan.

Money is nice, but a knowledgeable and creative staff is more important. Although one might expect the best practices in student services online to come from campuses with the largest budgets or the most sophisticated technology, that is not necessarily so. Some campus staffs are more student-centered and ready to embrace technology solutions. Some have tight or shrinking personnel budgets and see automating their services as the best way to continue to provide good or better service. Still others, especially those with staff wearing multiple hats and handling various services, see ways to reduce redundancy and deliver more efficient service to students by integrating them for online delivery.

Politics are alive and well on most campuses. Change occurs most easily when there is buy-in at the lowest levels and strong leadership or support from the top. On most campuses, there are early adopters who see ways to use technology and must convince others who may fear that they will lose touch with students or, worse, lose their jobs. Some simply want to do it the way it was always done, and until they retire it will be that way. The other common problem campuses report in this area is the autonomy of the IT staff, which can sometimes set priorities for implementing services online based on their own priorities, perceptions, or whims. On the flip side, some IT departments report that the other departments expect them to gather and maintain the information on the Web—a job that should be the responsibility of the service area instead.

The culture often shows. The language used on the institution's Web site and how the information is organized can tell a lot about the culture of the school. Some institutions have sites that display a cohesive understanding of the school's mission by a coordinated staff with a strong knowledge of its users' needs. The institutional brand and its promise of value are clear. There is a writing-style guide, a content-management software package is in place, and Web responsibilities are included in job descriptions. Other institutions have sites that display a hodgepodge of confusing paths and conflicting or outdated information. The navigation and look and feel are inconsistent. These institutions may have no leadership focus for the Web or suffer from insufficient funding. Regardless of the reason, today's students pick up on such variations quickly, and with a click of a mouse they find a school where they feel more comfortable.

Portals have been added but not integrated. Portals make it possible for schools to provide the customized and customizable service students really want. Yet many of these environments have simply been added onto the Web site so a student can conduct secure transactions. For example, a student may log in to check her grades or the status of her tuition payments, but find very little context for doing so. Frequently, she must return to the public site to find explanations or directions for next steps. This can be quite confusing. Perhaps the cause of this is that the portal is commonly thought of as a technology tool, rather than an information tool. It may be selected and implemented by the IT staff with little input from the student services staff. Once implemented, moreover, it is not uncommon for access to the student portal to be restricted to students—in other words, the student services staff cannot see what a student sees. By creating a guest student account with access to a dummy student record, institutions can help their student services staff develop a more effective environment. When the staff can work together on enhancing an enterprise-wide portal accessible via a single sign on, it can truly create a "high tech, high touch" experience for the student, a good basis for a long-term relationship.

Collaborative services are on the rise. Today, campuses are more willing to accept the idea that they do not have to be the provider of all services and are looking for ways to collaborate with others. This is seen as a way to reduce costs and provide a higher level of service—often Generation Three or above. This collaboration could be at the institution, system, or state level. For example, the chat online with a reference librarian at Cornell University may be staffed by a reference librarian at the University of Washington after 5:00 PM Eastern time. Other institutions license a service (most commonly, bookstore services, tutoring services, and internship and job placement services) from a professional association, consortia, or corporation. At the system and state level, these entities have worked with their members to design collaborative services. MnSCU's e-portfolio product and Kentucky's virtual library are examples.

An outside voice can make a difference. Student service staffs are often overloaded with day-to-day operations and may find it difficult to allocate time for an in-depth review of their services online. Even when they can find the time, they may not be able to shake the internal view or see what should be, rather than what is. Reports from focus groups with students and an objective third-party review of the student services online can provide a stimulus for more discussion and are likely to have more credibility among all the players.

Summary

Although student services online are still in their infancy, there are several characteristics that identify best practices in this arena. These include services that are student centered, blended, personalized, customized, customizable, convenient, and just in time. They also incorporate two-way communication strategies, integrated formats, and performance indicators. Using the Audit Tool, available through the Center for Transforming Student Services (www.centss. org), institutions can evaluate the comprehensiveness and quality of their online student services and identify where they are with the characteristics and critical components specific to each service. Early findings from research in best practices and use of the Audit Tool indicate that services within institutions are at different generational levels. Institutions with visions for services online, a creative staff, and a culture with the willingness to do things differently are most likely to create best practices in student services online.

Web Resources

Athabasca University. http://www.athabascau.ca/misc/expect
Arizona State University. http://www.asu.edu
Center for Transforming Student Services. http://www.centss.org
Mesa Community College. http://www.mc.maricopa.edu/
Minnesota State Colleges and Universities. http://www.efoliominnesota.com
Penn State University. http://www.psu.edu
Regis University. http://www.regis.edu
University of Arizona. http://www.career.arizona.edu/index.aspx
University of North Carolina, Greensboro. http://www.uncg.edu/students
WCET (Western Cooperative for Educational Telecommunications). http://www.wcet.info
Weber State University. http://www.Weber.edu
Western Governors University. http://www.wgu.edu

References

Burnett, D. J. *Innovation in Student Services: Planning for Models Blending High Touch/High Tech.* Washington, D.C.: Society for College and University Planning, 2002.
Western Cooperative for Educational Telecommunications (WCET). "Beyond the Administrative Core: Creating Web-Based Student Services for Online Learners." 2003. http://www.wcet.info/projects/laap. Accessed May 1, 2005.

PATRICIA A. (PAT) SHEA *is the assistant director of WCET and founder of the newly established Center for Transforming Student Services (CENTSS).*

3

Technology increasingly has become a driving force in the evolution of the student affairs profession. Student affairs professionals must have a baseline of technology skills to advance the student affairs profession.

Who Is Driving the Changing Landscape in Student Affairs?

Nessa Kleinglass

This chapter examines how the impact of technology is influencing the changes within student affairs, how technology is being used, what skills professionals must obtain, and the imperative leadership role that professionals must assume. The purpose of the chapter is to acknowledge the impact of technology in student affairs and challenge the professionals and practitioners within the field to be the drivers for the emerging path of the profession.

The future direction for the field of student affairs lies in the willingness of each professional to share his or her knowledge and understand the new dimensions being created by the driving force of technology. The limited participation of those who work in student affairs in connecting with issues related to technology has been noted by several authors (Upcraft, Terenzini, and Kruger, 1999; Love and Estanek, 2004). While technology is changing the fundamental way that students receive services and communicate, professionals have yet to demonstrate insight for the importance of their role and voice in the decisions around technology that affect student learning and development outcomes.

Student affairs professionals must begin to understand the importance of engaging as a change agent and participating in conversations about the use of technology within their field and institution. They need to guide and find a balance in the transformation from traditional face-to-face services to the digital environment, with the intention of establishing more robust and meaningful college experiences for students. In order to avoid the loss of trust or value in the overall purpose of student affairs, professionals who are

NEW DIRECTIONS FOR STUDENT SERVICES, no. 112, Winter 2005 © Wiley Periodicals, Inc.

the experts in student development must come forward and lead the evolving force of continuous change being initiated by technology.

The future direction of the student affairs profession will continue to be in jeopardy as long as people outside the field are allowed to establish protocol, strategies, goals, and a vision. While the academic community has been implementing the use of technology for learning in the classroom, student affairs professionals have minimally engaged in the conversation to demonstrate the significance of what they contribute to student learning. In order to maintain the value of the profession and fulfill the promise to students who rely on the student affairs practitioners to advocate and understand their out-of-classroom needs, action is needed now. Over time, the leap may be too vast, the voice may be too soft, and the opportunity to direct the vision of the field may be impossible.

The Impact of Technology

For many years the term *technology* was related to the application of science. Today, technology is defined as "innovation in action. It involves the generation of knowledge and processes to develop systems that solve problems and extend human capabilities" (International Technology Association, 1996, p. 16). People are responsible for thinking and expressing needs for which others build and develop technological solutions to fulfill a request or resolve a problem.

"Technology has existed since the first human began to seek control over the environment. The manipulation of stone, bone, hide, and metal led to an ever-increasing range of application. Thus began the exponential growth of technology, a growth that continues at an ever-increasing rate" today (Kozak and Robb, 1991, p. 30). Over the past centuries the economy moved from the agricultural age through the industrial age to the information age, in which knowledge has become the foundation and key to power (Tapscott, 1996). Today, technological influences are integrated and used by society more quickly than in the past (UCLA, 2003). Electricity was not used by the masses for more than forty-five years, while the gasoline automobile took fifty-five years to gain general acceptance, and mobile phones took thirteen years. In contrast, the Web took only four years to become integrated into people's lives (Milliron and Miles, 2000). Immense changes have taken place in a short time, with the introduction of the fax machine in 1977; the Internet in 1984; DVDs, enterprise, and content-management systems in 1996; and wireless computing in 2001. In changing how people communicate, the use of technology has outshined other inventions, such as the printing press, telephone, or television (Tapscott, 1996). In the beginning of the twenty-first century, the Internet is the foremost resource used for finding information (UCLA, 2003).

Many of the changes seen today were not envisioned a decade ago. American educational systems are being pulled into a more global world seeking different opportunities for learning. Information technology has altered our social institutions and changed how we work, play, and learn (Duderstadt, Atkins, and Van Houweling, 2002; International Technology Education Association, 1996). How these changes will evolve and what new mechanisms will be introduced are unclear, but certainly a strong need exists to address the transformation that is taking place. Educators must prepare to have the capacity for dealing with upcoming change. The ability to understand the ramifications of information technology in relation to student development and the skills to use technological tools to accomplish goals and fulfill work responsibilities are paramount, especially within student affairs.

The technological expectations of students, though powerful and uncomfortable at times, are forcing a new direction regarding the provision of services, communication, and sharing of information. Student development and growth are core values for those who work in student affairs. The professionals in the field are noting change and are beginning to realize the need to acknowledge the impact of technology (Kleinglass, 2004). Some experts in the field are becoming conscious of the need to guide the direction for the use of technology in a manner that encourages student growth and learning, provides balance, and positively reflects the needs of students in building a personal community, academic success, and personal growth.

Today's college students consider the Internet an indispensable tool for their educational experience and demonstrate the impact of technology each day by using technology tools to communicate with family, friends, and college professors; to perform research and complete classroom requirements; for entertainment; and to enhance overall personal and social learning experiences (Jones, 2003; NSSE, 2003). Technology "that is expanding our ability to create, transfer, and apply knowledge by factors of 100 to 1,000 every decade" will have a "profound impact on both the mission and the function of the university" and student college experience (Tapscott, 1996, p. ix).

Within the past five years, intense changes have occurred in the way students access and use technology for learning, communicating, and retrieving information. Many students use the Internet as a source for meeting or conversing with others. They listen to music, watch movies, and play games. In fact, 20 percent of college students feel that gaming helps them continue and find new friendships (Jones, 2003). Students increasingly use technology for course registration, textbook purchases, and library research as well as to talk with professors, access financial aid, and find billing information. Students can register a club or organization online and often can promote an organization through the college servers. Students can purchase tickets for campus events or sign up for their cap and gown online. Many campuses seek outside vendors and purchase rights to Internet resources that enable students to use self-help guides to determine if they have a medical issue and should see a health professional. At some institutions, students can set up appointments with a counselor, nurse, or advisor using online scheduling software. Interactive software is available that enables students to have virtual tours of residence of halls, to choose roommates in similar formats to using an online dating service, and to select residence-hall rooms similar to selecting seats on an airplane. Nine out of every ten college students own a cellular phone. More than 88 percent of four-year, full-time undergraduate college students own a computer, and 17 percent own more than one computer. In fall 2004, students spent about fifteen hours a week online, which is 42 percent more than in 2001 (Student Monitor, 2005).

Enterprise systems and campus portals are enabling online registration, applications, and business processes to be personalized. The availability of student information is more readily accessible to staff. Judicial issues are being initiated and processed through Web-accessible software, and reports and information on sanctions can be connected through campus systems. Mini-workshops and seminars can be available for students and parents on myriad topics. Students can sign up for career seminars, résumé evaluation, or meetings with potential employers.

Campus administrators are realizing the importance of the Web as a resource that unlocks internal and external exposure of the institution. Campuses are branding the college image through the development of consistently imaged Web sites that are more personal and interactive, and that provide updated information and access to selected services twenty-four hours a day. They are recognizing the importance of simplifying the navigation, categorizing information, and portraying an image that reflects the goals and mission of the institution. Web sites are being seen as an investment and resource for external communities to learn about the institution and for the institution to demonstrate accountability and value to communities outside the university, including prospective students and alumni.

By the middle of first decade of the twenty-first century, the infusion of technology in higher learning environments is apparent. The changes imposed by technology have been evolving. The message is clear that the infusion of technology will continue to affect higher education learning environments. Along with students, faculty, and administrators, student affairs professionals must be certain their voice is heard.

Staff Technology Skills

While student affairs professionals are experts in understanding the types of traditional services and activities that increase college success and retention, they are far from adept in using and understanding the technological tools that are affecting how connections occur in the changing environment of the twenty-first century. The use of technology within higher education is becoming stronger over time, and the expectations of students more demanding. Meanwhile, the involvement of student affairs professionals remains limited. While the need for action, intervention, and collaboration has been stated, few specific guides or models have been established and shared as a starting point. With this in mind, the following information and model is presented as a tool for conversation, expansion, and adaptation.

In July 2003, the student affairs staff at a four-year higher education institution in the Midwest were asked to participate in a survey to evaluate how staff use technology within student affairs. Half the staff had been at the institution for fewer than six years, but the majority of the staff were seasoned employees, having worked for ten or more years within the field of student affairs. The first section of the survey was separated into three parts that referred to the use of technology tools, software, and online activities. For each of these parts, the participant was asked about the frequency with which he or she uses the tool, the importance of the tool for his or her job, and his or her level of proficiency in its use (Kleinglass, 2003).

From this study, a proficiency model was designed as a foundation to prepare staff with the basic skills to use technology in their work today and with the intent that this foundation would enable them to have a base from which to enhance their skills as technology demands change. The study showed that desktop computers and copy machines were the most important tools. While everyone used them and found them important, only about half of the staff expressed feeling very proficient with these tools. Browsers, calendars, and word-processing applications were used by more than 90 percent of the staff, with word-processing software designated as the most important for job performance. Almost everyone expressed feeling some level of proficiency with word-processing tools, but only 50 percent of those surveyed felt highly proficient. The calendar was the most-used software, but only one-third of the staff expressed confidence or proficiency in using this tool. While browsers were used by more than 90 percent of staff, only 28 percent of the staff felt highly proficient with them. Although all staff used e-mail and performed Internet searches, and considered these functions to be important in performing their jobs, only 70 percent felt highly proficient using e-mail and 39 percent doing Internet searches. Few staff used instant messaging or chat groups at work. Online classes, meetings, and conferences appeared to have little significance for staff. PDAs, digital imaging, and discussion boards were designated as important tools but were not being used regularly in the workplace.

Many staff articulated a need to improve skills. Overall, about two-thirds of staff felt they had some skills to use technology tools required for their job, but less than 75 percent of the staff expressed feeling very proficient in using the tools or software, or performing activities included in the survey. At the time of the survey, 71 percent of the staff were accessing e-mail from home and 83 percent expressed interest in accessing their computer files from home, a function not yet available through the campus systems. Eighty-eight percent of the staff supported the need to personalize the way that the Internet is used to provide services to students. Only half the staff felt that they received enough training for the technology tools that they need to use while working. Interestingly, 13 percent of the staff spent less than 25 percent of their day on the computer, 13 percent spent more than 75 percent of their day on the computer, and approximately 40 percent of the staff spent more than half their day on the computer (Kleinglass, 2003). With minimal professional development and training, staff within student affairs should be able to increase their effectiveness using technology and align more readily with student technology skills.

The findings for the tools, software, and online activities were imbedded in a graphic that can be envisioned as a three-dimensional object that allows additional tiers to be expanded outward building on necessary skills *as new skills evolve,* as depicted in Figure 3.1. The four categories of limited, valuable, basic, and necessary apply to the importance to the job of the tools being used. Table 3.1 provides a key describing those proficiency levels. The content within each tier is adjustable to the dynamic environment of technology, as information within each tier of the diagram is movable and thus can be adapted to meet individual institutional standards or fluctuate between levels as the need for specific technology skills changes.

Beyond developing the skills to use tools, professionals need to comprehend and envision how technology can be used. Staff need to incorporate their knowledge of sociology, social psychology, cultural anthropology, economics, and organization theory (Curry, 2002). They need to remove the fears and phobias related to technology by evaluating and understanding the influence, function, and role of technology with regard to student learning. Professionals can begin to influence and guide the role of technology within student affairs when they can articulate how technology influences outcomes, actions, expectations, and student behaviors. By understanding the conceptual and functional impact of technology on institutional goals, quality of service, and resources, and by being able to differentiate between student interests and needs, student affairs staff can provide information to guide administrators in making effective decisions that positively affect retention, use of resources, and the student experience. More than ever, professionals need to improve their skills for developing partnerships, building collaborative efforts, advocating for students, and incorporating the student voice into campus decisions. The optimal transition from traditional to balanced, Web-based services and learning opportunities will require multiple departmental discussions, participation at all levels of staff, and collaborative decision

Table 3.1. Key to Proficiency Model Levels

Tiers	Definition	Items reported by
Necessary	Mandatory proficiency for all	100%–90%
Basic	Supports overall ability to perform technology tasks	89%–75%
Valuable	Designated specialists or those who use specified technologies	74%–41%
Limited	Designated for elite users, for use outside the workplace, or for the creation of new technologies	40%–0%

Figure 3.1. Proficiency Model—Tools Used and Importance to Job

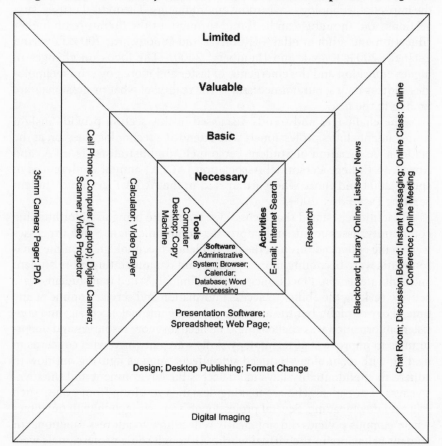

making. Competent staff who are flexible and willing to dedicate their time and effort for using, functionally understanding, and envisioning the impact of technology in student learning and development can be the drivers of the evolving design of the student affairs profession.

Challenges and Trends

Underlying the basic goals and values of student affairs is an emerging understanding that the way services are being provided to students is changing and will continue to evolve in the coming years. The demand for change comes from the importance of knowledge in today's global environment, new challenges in higher education, the changing student population, and the impact of technology in learning environments. Theoretical causes, suggestions, and thoughts can be found throughout the literature on higher education and student affairs (Komives and Woodward, 2003; Love and Estanek, 2004; Kvavik and Handberg, 2000). The focus on changes in higher education and the emergence of faster and more powerful technologies address issues, but not necessarily the reality, of what professionals are finding in the field.

The challenges and trends discussed in this section provide insight from student affairs professionals who attended a technology session at the National Association of Student Personnel Administrators (NASPA) and American College Personnel Association (ACPA) annual conferences in spring 2004 and those who participated in the ACPA Electronic Student Services Task Force 2004.

Practitioners stated that technology tools were being used for building community, assessment, and improving communication. Some processes were being enhanced through the use of blended technologies. Online environments were becoming more dynamic and demonstrating more student and staff interaction. Practitioners overwhelmingly stated that students were actively seeking the ability to access information and services online at any time of day or night, but the ability to provide continual, accurate, and consistent information was challenging. The need for more resources and opportunities to improve staff technology skills were entwined with concerns in dealing with technology-induced side effects, such as figuring out how to adhere to confidentiality laws in an accessible environment and the invasiveness of outsiders who are making demands resulting from events such as illegal downloading. Several professionals were struggling with outcomes where campus policies did not clearly reflect how to address sanctions for student behaviors in the virtual world. Although some professionals were anxious about the loss of personal contact with students, they were beginning to realize that the key is to guide universities in finding the balance between traditional and digital connections that are meaningful for students and assist them in reaching their full potential.

Professionals are looking for more resources and support from campus administration. They want opportunities to be included in conversations that address students and technology, both on campuses and with colleagues in the field. At the same time, they are struggling with their own limitations, and many are seeking the expertise of those who can build a bridge between the student learning and development and technology within higher education. They seek answers and models where minimal exploration and little measurement have been done.

The continued intervention of technology and increased student use of technology tools reveal how communication, learning, and student lifestyles are changing. In 2004, students reported spending about 15.1 hours online communicating, studying, and shopping—42 percent more time than in fall

2001 (Student Monitor, 2005). Nine out of every ten college students own a cell phone at an average cost of $56 per month (Student Monitor, 2005). During the past decade, a greater number of students each year have been using online services to research and apply to colleges, register for classes, and purchase textbooks. Web portals, blending technologies, and increasing personalization of the Web are occurring. In addition to the increased organization, customizations, and personalization of information, Web sites are being designed to reflect a consistent image that reflects each institution's mission and goals.

While each college or university struggles to find a niche in the changing educational environment, one common element remains: the need to focus on the student and his or her college experience. No longer can student affairs professionals act independently. Information is knowledge, and student affairs divisions need to focus on building environments that can explain the positive effects of services and activities on student learning to others in the educational community. The challenge is to understand how to demonstrate accountability for what is accomplished and to determine productive and collaborative alternatives and resources for serving diverse populations of students. Awareness of the institutional environment as well as societal and student expectations must be understood and used to shape the future of the profession. "Students need more than just knowledge as information. They need the ability to understand and apply the knowledge in order to gain wisdom. Wisdom refers to knowledge infused with experience, perspective, and content" (Woodward, Love, and Komives, 2000, p. 8).

Technology-driven change affects the activities of the university, including the development of community, sharing of experiences, and learning (Duderstadt, Atkins, and Van Houweling, 2002). Discussions and actions by those in the field are necessary to guide a direction that benefits, strengthens, and clarifies the role of student affairs within educational institutions.

At the ACPA annual conference in Nashville in 2005, eighteen professionals gathered to discuss technology. Most participants came to learn how others were addressing issues related to technology. Propelled by illegal downloading and social networking through Web sites such as facebook.com, they realized the need to become proactive rather than reactive and were looking for ways to have dialogue with colleagues. In summary, they were searching to discover the values of technology as a tool for communication and learning, to connect with students, and for opportunities to broaden their own skills and knowledge to be effective leaders in the field and on their campus.

Role of Leadership

Traditionally, the effective student affairs practitioner is a strong communicator and good listener who can motivate others, plan, implement, and deal with conflict and crisis situations (Woodward, Love, and Komives,

2000). The student affairs practitioner is expected to positively influence a student's intellectual and personal growth, enhance self-esteem, and develop leadership skills (Miller, 2003). As caring adults dedicated to the social and psychological growth of students and the promise to enhance the college experience, many professionals have failed to address, focus, and connect with the effects of technology-driven environments, but rather leave the planning and strategies for implementation to others. Consequently, the destiny of a large portion of student learning is being left in the hands of others who may not have the expertise and understanding of student interest, desires, and needs. Before the opportunity to contribute to the foundation and direction of student leadership and development passes, professionals have a responsibility and obligation to engage in leadership roles.

Leadership is a word that implies action. The literature is full of information on the characteristics of leaders and types of leadership. In order to simplify and provide meaning, the following concepts have been selected to initiate thought and philosophy and to encourage professionals to think about ways to influence the outcomes for using technology in student affairs.

As leaders, individuals or groups "influence the thoughts, behaviors, and/or feelings of others," and telling of stories is at the heart of leadership (Gardner and Hobbs, 1995, p. 6). Practitioners need to begin to tell stories about their experiences with students in relation to the influences of technology. What about the student who went online and took a self-assessment that led her to seek counseling? What about the student who became active in a service learning activity after reading about the adventure online? What about the roommates who could not get along and argued in virtual meetings while sitting in the same room? What about the adult learner with a low level of technology proficiency who fell behind in his class and almost left college? Student affairs professionals have a multitude of stories, but who hears the stories, the successes, and the challenges that practitioners face in striving to enhance the college experience, improve retention, and develop leaders? By sharing stories in the context of technological need, impact, and outcomes, professionals can begin to take a leadership role.

Leadership is a "shared, interactive, culturally framed activity" (Bensimon and Neumann, 1994, pp. xi-xii) in which teams bring together diverse thoughts. Certainly, the student affairs professionals working to develop the whole student must consult, collaborate, and establish new approaches in changing times. Working together can lead to more viable outcomes for the direction and transformation of the field and more meaningful and effective outcomes for students. Working together will require each person to engage and share, reflect and interact, and be open to new approaches. Professionals need to work together to ensure that their voice is heard on campuses and in national forums and discussions.

Professionals today must have the courage to step forward. Courage means having the nerve to overcome fears around technology and do what needs to be done. Courage means having the willingness to do things differently, to accept that resistance comes with change, and to stay committed. Being a courageous leader means accepting responsibility and having the fortitude to reach goals and accept change. Consistency and focus on goals and values are important, as is the appreciation of others. Courageous leaders are caring yet able to articulate a clear vision and expectation. Communication is paramount and requires opportunity to share knowledge, provide feedback, and accept thought processes and differences in people. A courageous leader is optimistic, able to build trust, set examples, and address issues (Cottrell and Harvey, 2004).

Student affairs professionals must envision themselves as the leaders and experts who have the knowledge and thus power to direct the inevitable changes in the profession. They need to recognize the looming risk as those who are not experts in student development are beginning to affect the direction of the future of the profession. The ability to transform the field is still open to those who are willing to show the spirit and courage to step forward.

The Future of the Field of Student Affairs

Technology is the catalyst that is changing the way connections and learning occur with college students inside and outside the classroom. The pervasiveness of technology tools is ever-increasing, and the thrust and magnitude of change are becoming stronger and more evident with time and affecting the performance and function of the university (Duderstadt, Atkins, and Van Houweling, 2002). Digital technologies have been transforming the way universities function, but the use and impact of the technologies are only part of the equation.

The main issue is not technology, but people. The human element is both the creative genius and the inhibiter of technology that has become a powerful force. Professionals must train new staff, build partnerships within the college community and others in the field across the country, be inclusive and collaborative, and educate administrators. Professionals in the field must articulate a foundation, envision the direction and goals for the next decade, and establish a process that enables professionals to fulfill the void in leadership around technology for student development and learning outside the classroom. The role of student affairs professionals is to find a balance in order to affect the development, learning, and growth of students today and in the future. They need to take the responsibility for ensuring that the college experience will continue to be meaningful for all students.

Student affairs professionals have arrived at a critical crossroad in their profession. If they are to take a leadership and collaborative role in the future direction of technology within student affairs, they must become proficient in using the tools and understanding their function. They need encouragement, training, and cultures that support creative thought and action and that reward new ideas, collaborative conversations, and partnerships across campus. In order to lead, professionals must understand the impact of technology, the implications for technology-driven change, and the challenges and trends facing divisions of student affairs. They must learn to think creatively about how technology can be used to solve problems and how to avoid problems from using technology. They must develop skills for understanding the role of the human, functional, and technical elements related to technology. Using their knowledge from sociology, psychology, and student development, professionals must build a vision for the future in collaboration with faculty, administrators, and technology staff. As those who work closely with students, they must become a conduit for hearing the student voice and sharing the students' expectations and needs with others in the campus community.

Who is driving the changing landscape in student affairs? People are. In order to state clearly that the professionals and practitioners within the field are leading the change in collaboration with students, faculty, and administrators, the following must occur:

Staff need to be active users of the Web, engage in online conversations, and interact with students. They need to hear the students' technological expectations and advocate for their needs.

Content that is important for students must be available at all hours, online, clear, and up-to-date. In order to accomplish this collaborative effort, an empowering and trusting relationship must exist between the division and those responsible for the technical support of systems.

In order to demonstrate value, professionals need to access and understand how to use technology tools for assessments and relate the information to outcomes, activities, and funding.

Student Affairs professionals need to become advisors for decision makers regarding the use of technology for student communication and development.

Staff must become highly proficient in using the technology tools and software and performing the online activities required to do their job effectively.

In order to provide effective guidance for outsourcing and working with vendors, staff must be knowledgeable about the purpose and function of technologies on campus and be able to demonstrate value for fiscal commitments.

Training, whether full-day events or short, bag-lunch sessions, to understand the function of technology tools or enhance present technology skills must be developed and offered in formats that fit staff schedules and institutional budgets.

The use of technology and understanding about the function of technology must be integrated into the curriculum of professional degree programs.

Research and data that demonstrate the value of student affairs work must be encouraged, supported, and shared.

Professional organizations that must step forward as models for using technology and provide forums for professionals to become knowledgeable about technology, to determine the best use and function, and to share best practices and models from the field and professionals are obligated to participate and share their stories.

The topic of technology in student affairs can no longer be ignored or allowed to flow in and out of conversations and job descriptions.

Those who work in student affairs must be courageous, open, and flexible communicators willing to facilitate, act, and function in an environment of change with the purpose of enhancing each student's experience on campus. Technology must be a focus connecting to the values and practices of the field and placed on the student affairs map.

References

Bensimon, E. M., and Neumann, A. *Redesigning Collegiate Leadership: Teams and Teamwork in Higher Education.* Baltimore, Md.: Johns Hopkins University Press, 1994.

Cottrell, D., and Harvey, E. *Leadership Courage: Leadership Strategies for Individual and Organizational Success.* Dallas, Tex.: Walk the Talk, 2004.

Curry, J. R. "The Organizational Challenge: IT and Revolution in Higher Education." In R. H. Katz (ed.), *Web Portals and Higher Education: Technologies to Make IT Personal.* San Francisco: Jossey-Bass, 2002.

Duderstadt, J. J., Atkins, D. E., and Van Houweling, D. *Higher Education in the Digital Age: Technology Issues and Strategies for American Colleges and Universities.* Westport, Conn.: American Council on Education and Praeger, 2002.

Gardner, H., and Hobbs, E. A. *Leading Minds: An Anatomy of Leadership.* New York: BasicBooks, 1995.

International Technology Education Association. *Technology for All Americans: A Rationale and Structure for the Study of Technology.* Reston, Va.: International Technology Association, 1996.

Jones, S. "Let the Games Begin: Gaming Technology and Entertainment Among College Students." Pew Internet & American Life Project, July 6, 2003. http://www.pewinternet.org/PPF/r/93/report_display.asp. Accessed May 2005.

Kleinglass, N. *How Staff Use Technology in Student Affairs.* Unpublished study, 2003.

Kleinglass, N. "Managing Technology and the Role of Leadership." Roundtable at the American College Personnel Association Annual Conference, Nashville, 2005.

Komives, S. R., and Woodward, D. B., Jr. *Student Services: A Handbook for the Profession.* (4th ed.) San Francisco: Jossey-Bass, 2003.

Kozak, M. R., and Robb, J. "Education About Technology." In M. J. Dyrenfurth and M. R. Kozak (eds.), *Technological Literacy: Council on Technology Teacher Education 40th Yearbook.* Westerville, Ohio: Glencoe, 1991.

Kvavik, R. B., and Handberg, M. N. "Transforming Student Services." *EDUCAUSE Quarterly,* 2000, 23(2), 30–37.

Love, P., and Estanek, S. *Rethinking Student Affairs Practice.* San Francisco: Jossey-Bass, 2004.

Miller, T. K., (ed.). *CAS: The Book of Professional Standards for Higher Education.* Washington, D.C.: Council of Advancement of Standards in Higher Education, 2003.

Milliron, M. D., and Miles, C. L. "Education in a Digital Democracy: Leading the Charge for Learning About, with, and Beyond Technology." *EDUCAUSE,* Nov.-Dec. 2000, pp. 50–59.

NSSE (National Survey of Student Engagement). "NSSE 2003 Overview." http://www.indiana.edu/~nsse/nsse_2003/overview_2003.htm. Accessed April 2005.

Student Monitor. *2005.* Press releases 02, 09 and 10. http://www.studentmonitor.com/press/. Accessed May 2005.

Tapscott, D. *The Digital Economy: Promise and Peril in the Age of Networked Intelligence.* New York: McGraw-Hill, 1996.

UCLA News. "Internet Peaks as America's Most Important Source of Information." *UCLA News,* Jan. 31, 2003. http://newsroom.ucla.edu/page.asp?id=3856. Accessed May 2005.

Upcraft, M. L., Terenzini, P. T. and Kruger, K. "Looking Beyond the Horizon: Trends Shaping Student Affairs." Washington, D.C.: American College Personnel Association, 1999. http://www.acpa.nche.edu/seniorscholars/trends/trends5.htm. Accessed April 2, 2003.

Woodward, D. B., Jr., Love, P., and Komives, S. R. "Leadership and Management Issues for a New Century." In D. B. Woodward, Jr., P. Love, and S. R. Komives (eds.), New Directions for Student Services, no. 92. San Francisco: Jossey Bass, 2000.

NESSA KLEINGLASS was formerly director of special projects at the University of Saint Thomas.

4

In order to understand and meet the needs of the distance learning population, student affairs administrators must partner with our colleagues in the fields of technology and distance education. A study of distance learners at North Carolina State University provides information and opportunities for strengthening those partnerships.

Assessing the Needs of Distance Learners: A Student Affairs Perspective

Leslie A. Dare, Lisa P. Zapata, Amanda G. Thomas

The convergence of technology, student affairs, and distance education has begun but is not yet complete. Given the ubiquitous nature of technology, the growth of distance education enrollments, and the role of student affairs in student learning and success, these three fields are now inextricably connected and form a triangular relationship (see Figure 4.1).

Currently, the strongest of these three relationships is between technology and distance education. Technology is the fuel on which distance education runs and is a primary focal point in virtually all distance education professional organizations and publications. Likewise, distance education is a regular feature in the technology field.

The relationship between technology and student affairs, while not anywhere near that of technology and distance education, is strengthening. Technology has received significant attention in the field of student affairs through its organizations, publications, and professional preparation graduate programs. While not a regular feature, student affairs and its various units do receive some attention in the technology field, particularly related to student conduct, records, policy, and security.

The weakest relationship is between student affairs and distance education. Distance education, while becoming a somewhat more visible topic, has not been featured in student affairs to the same degree as have technology or other topics. Likewise, student affairs is rarely mentioned in the field of distance education and is usually limited to the discussion of a narrow set of student services. Herein lies a significant gap: the triangle of student affairs, technology, and distance education is not complete because the connection

Figure 4.1. Relationship among Technology, Student Affairs, and Distance Learners

between student affairs and distance education is still in the early stages of development. However, it is encouraging that both professions—distance education and student affairs—are aware of this gap and are looking for ways to strengthen the bond. This triangular relationship highlights several issues that must be addressed by student affairs administrators, such as the role of student affairs in serving distance learners, the use of technology by distance learners and by student affairs offices, and the needs of the distance learning population.

Distance learners are a segment of today's college student population that can no longer be ignored by the student affairs profession. The most recent government data indicate that 56 percent of all degree-granting institutions offered at least one distance education course in 2000–2001; among these institutions, 34 percent offered degree programs designed to be completed totally through distance education. Distance education now has significant alliances with industry and the military and is viewed as one important solution to overall enrollment growth in higher education (Howell, Williams, and Lindsay, 2003). The impact is a shift in higher education from a campus-centric model, which is constrained by place and time, with control in the hands of administrators and faculty, to a consumer-centric model, where control is shared with the student and without the time and place constraints (Twigg and Oblinger, 1996; Beaudoin, 2003).

At North Carolina State University, the historic and projected growth of the distance learning population has mimicked the national trend, having started with video-based courses, adding Internet-based courses, eventually developing full degree programs, and anticipating more than 15 percent growth annually (North Carolina State University, 2005). In 1997, the North Carolina state legislature designated funding for distance education as one solution to the tremendous increase in college enrollment expected in the state. This funding trickled down to the Division of Student Affairs, resulting in the creation of a full-time professional staff position responsible for helping the many units in the Division serve the distance learning population through its diverse courses, programs, and services.

Literature Review

A significant area of growth in literature about distance learning in higher education focuses on student services. Support for distance learners is emphasized in publications by professional organizations and associations, primarily in the fields of distance education and technology. All regional accrediting bodies (Council of Regional Accrediting Commissions, 2001) and the American Council on Education (2002) have issued guidelines regarding distance education that highlight student support as an integral element.

While the topics of student support and student services appear with increasing frequency in the literature, the provision of student services is reported to be a significant but underdeveloped component of distance education programs (Peters, 1998; McLendon and Cronk, 1999; Husmann and Miller, 2001; Levy and Beaulieu, 2003; Levy, 2003). Student services for distance education is also an area that has only recently seen empirical study and is still quite lacking (Visser and Visser, 2000; LaPadula, 2003).

Two administrative philosophies for serving the distance learning population emerge from the literature: separate services for distance learners that exist in parallel to services provided for on-campus students, and integrated services that serve both the distance education and on-campus populations. Separate services seem to proliferate as a reaction to needs identified after distance education programs are established (Blimling and Whitt, 1999). This approach is also advocated as a deliberate one to ensure that the special needs of distance learners are met (Connick, 2001). However, others contend that integrating services for distance learners with services provided for on-campus students will result in a more comprehensive services package and make efficient use of resources (Rinear, 2003; Meyers and Ostash, 2004; Floyd and Casey-Powell, 2004). Kretovics (2003) asserts, "This view of separate but equal services should be unacceptable to current student affairs practitioners" (p. 11).

One major model for defining the scope of services for distance learners emerges in both the literature and in institutional practice and can be described as an enrollment management-plus model. Included in this model are the typical enrollment-management services, such as admissions, financial aid, and registration, in addition to basic academic resources, such as libraries, academic advising, and technical support. These represent the minimal transactional services required for students to be enrolled and complete a distance education course and for which technology has been used to adapt existing services to extend the provision to the distance learning population. This limited set is very often the extent of services found in the literature and offered in practice (Western Cooperative for Educational Telecommunications, 2003; LaPadula, 2004). Even the eight regional accrediting bodies use this model in their "Best Practices for Electronically Offered Degree and Certificate Programs" (Southern Association of Colleges and Schools, 2000). There has been a recent trend to include tutoring, career counseling, and bookstore services in research and in practice (Levy and Beaulieu, 2003; Floyd and Casey-Powell, 2004). While some researchers have been looking beyond this somewhat limited model and examining other services and activities as well, such as student health, student government, personal counseling, orientation, and virtual communities (Hirt, Cain, Bryant, and Williams, 2003; LaPadula, 2003; Rinear, 2003; Meyers and Ostash, 2004), no studies could be identified involving institutions that offer the full array of student affairs programs and activities to the distance learning population.

There is some evidence that distance learners, who tend to be older and have work and family commitments (Kretovics, 2003; Moe, 2002; Howell, Williams, and Lindsay, 2003), do not desire these services (Hirt, Cain, Bryant, and Williams, 2003). However, the distance learner population will see growth in the traditional college demographic group as higher education enrollments grow overall and institutions continue to use distance education as a means to meet enrollment projections.

While the body of research is growing, there is one significant omission of key importance from the student affairs perspective. Missing from much of the earlier distance education literature is the connection between success and a sense of connection with other students and the institution. One exception is Krauth and Carbajal (1999), who find that sense of connection is strongly tied to retention, completion, and satisfaction. A widely accepted concept in the student affairs profession is that traditional on-campus students benefit from being engaged in campus life and feeling connected to various aspects of the institution (Pascarella and Terenzini, 1991). This benefit may also extend to distance learners, as evidence mounts that these students are more successful when provided with support services (Dirr, 1999; Levy and Beaulieu, 2003). The term *student services* itself is often referenced to include transactional services that are necessary for the student to conduct business with the institution (enrollment management) and academic services (plus). The term can be considered exclusive of the type of programming available to traditional on-campus students that enhance their sense of connection. Examples include student organizations; support centers for marginalized student populations, such as women, gay-lesbian-transgendered, and African-American students; health education; arts programs; student government; leadership programs; recreation programs; and student activities.

More recent research has observed the importance of sense of connection for distance learners as the student affairs profession seeks to understand its role in serving this population. Meyers and Ostash (2004) point to the value of online communities to nurture distance learners' sense of inclusion. Floyd and Casey-Powell (2004) include "social support services" as one type of "student support services" available to distance learners, and "fostering sense of belonging" is included in the "Inclusive Student Services Process Model" they articulate (p. 59). Kretovics (2003) includes "the creation of community" as a primary recommendation for student affairs professionals in serving the distance learning population (p. 5) and suggests that some of the lessons learned in serving commuter students in the 1970s and 1980s may be helpful in serving distance learners.

There does seem to be a concern in the student affairs profession that interpersonal interactions are being sacrificed in order to achieve efficiency in providing student services. Although distance makes in-person interactions difficult, the Internet provides flexibility in communication via e-mail, instant messaging, online forms, and video conferencing. These Internet solutions are welcomed, but with some trepidation. Meyers and Ostash (2004) suggest that practitioners should deliberately plan which services will be contact and which will be self-serve. A distance learning task force convened by the National Association of Student Personnel Administrators (NASPA, 2000) contends that distance learners may not experience the same socialization process as their on-campus counterparts. The term "high tech—high touch," first coined by John Nesbitt (1982), still resonates for student affairs practitioners who are looking for a balanced approach in using technology to serve both distance learners and on-campus learners.

In an effort to understand better the role of the Division of Student Affairs in serving the distance learners at North Carolina State University, a survey was conducted to gauge several aspects of the distance education experience. For the purposes of the study, the term *distance learners* was used to describe those students at NC State University who were enrolled only in distance education course(s) at the time of the study. The term *on-campus learners* described those students who were enrolled only in on-campus courses at the time of the study.

Method

This quantitative study was designed to compare the responses of distance learners at NC State University with a matched group of on-campus learners.

Participants. A total of 2,077 students—the entire distance learning population at NC State University—was surveyed in the fall semester of 2003. Of these, 778 students participated, for a response rate of 37.4 percent. A control group of on-campus students was selected based on matching characteristics of gender and ethnicity. A total of 6,190 on-campus students was surveyed, and 1,962 participated for a response rate of 31.6 percent.

Instrumentation. The research team collected feedback from all student affairs offices and other units providing services to students to develop the survey instrument. The survey was distributed to both on-campus and distance learners in an attempt to learn whether there were any differences between these student groups regarding their knowledge, use, and need of the various courses, services, and programs in student affairs. Students were asked to rate importance, satisfaction, and likeliness on a four-point Likert-type scale (1 = Very Unimportant, 4 = Very Important; 1 = Very Unsatisfied, 4 = Very Satisfied; 1 = Very Unlikely, 4 = Very Likely).

The survey was divided into five sections:

- Specific experiences as distance learners, including their primary reasons for taking a distance education course, the frequency of campus visits and the reasons for those visits
- Technology, including skills, type of computer, and type, frequency, and location of Internet connection
- Sense of connection with others at the University
- Preferences for communicating with NC State University's various departments, programs and services
- Importance and satisfaction of each of the available services and programs
- Importance and likelihood of use of services and programs not available to distance learners.

The survey distributed to the on-campus control group included the same questions as the distance learner survey, with the exception of the sections regarding the distance learning experience and likelihood of using services and programs currently not available to distance learners.

Procedure. The surveys were administered electronically to both on-campus students and distance learners. Using a homegrown bulk e-mail system, an initial invitation was sent that contained a hypertext link to a web-based survey. A paper version was available on request. After the initial invitation, two follow-up e-mails were sent to non-respondents to encourage the completion of the survey. The distance learners received an additional follow-up from their faculty encouraging them to complete the survey. A cash incentive was promoted in the original invitation and subsequent e-mails to enhance the response rate.

Analysis. The data were analyzed using descriptive statistics of the variables, such as frequencies, as well as inferential statistics. Two-way analysis of variance was used to determine if there were statistical differences between the means of selected variables. An alpha value of .05 was chosen to determine if differences were statistically significant. R-squares were examined to indicate the strengths of the relationships.

Results

The results of the survey underscored significant differences between distance and on-campus learners.

Experiences as a Distance Learner. The first section of the survey, which was not included in the version distributed to on-campus students, examined the specific experiences of distance learners. When distance learners were asked why they took distance-education courses, the most frequently cited reason was to accommodate work schedules (72.6 percent), followed, in order, by family obligations (42.3 percent), live too far (42.1 percent), prefer distance education (24.7 percent), financial (16 percent), other (12.8 percent), course not available on campus (4.2 percent), and on-campus section full (2.8 percent). The survey also asked how often and why distance learners came to campus. With respect to frequency, 40.9 percent reported that they never came to campus, 31.8 percent came once or twice a semester, 18.2 percent monthly, 6.3 percent weekly, and 2.8 percent daily. Respondents gave varying reasons for why they came to campus, including to take tests and exams (34.5 percent), purchase textbooks and supplies (32.5 percent), meet instructor (16.6 percent), use libraries (15.9 percent), meet advisor (11.5 percent), pay for courses (11.3 percent), register for courses (9.8 percent), attend NC State events (7.9 percent), use computer resources (6.8 percent), and get ID card (5.1 percent).

Technology. The second section of the survey addressed the use of technology. While both distance learners and on-campus learners were asked these questions, only results for distance learners are reported here. Distance learners were overwhelmingly satisfied with their overall computer skills, with 96.4 percent indicating that they were either satisfied or very satisfied. When asked where they connect to the Internet, distance learners most frequently cited home (90.2 percent), followed, in order, by work (54.9 percent), NC State campus (9.4 percent), public library (4.7 percent), and other (7.4 percent). To connect to the Internet at home, 30.8 percent of distance learners reported using a telephone modem and 62.4 percent used a high-speed connection device. When asked about the quality of their Internet connection at home, 68.3 percent described their connection as good or excellent, 19.8 percent as adequate, and 6.4 percent as poor. Less than one percent said their connection was unacceptable.

Sense of Connection. The third section of the survey asked students to report their sense of connection with various components of university life. The survey examined students' sense of connection at the micro and macro levels (see Table 4.1). Respondents were asked to rate the importance of each component assessing a sense of connection, as well as their satisfaction with each. Choices ranged from one to four, from Very Unimportant to Very Important.

With the exception of sense of connection with "My instructor," there were statistically significant differences between distance learners and on-campus learners for the importance of each component that assessed the sense of connection. On-campus students consistently reported statistically significant higher levels of importance. With respect to satisfaction, there

Table 4.1. Sense of Connection

Component	Importance		Satisfaction	
	DE Pure	Campus	DE Pure	Campus
Students in my [DE] courses	2.53	3.10*	3.01	2.98
Students in general	2.08	2.87*	3.07	2.93*
My instructor	3.63	3.60	3.18	2.96*
My academic adviser	2.92	3.47*	3.06	2.97
My academic department	2.96	3.44*	3.08	2.98*
Faculty in general	2.82	3.12*	3.09	2.90*
NC State University	3.03	3.38*	3.16	3.08*

$*p < .05$

were statistically significant differences for each item except "Students in my [distance] course(s)" and "My academic adviser." Unlike importance, where on-campus students reported higher levels of importance, distance learners reported statistically significant higher levels of satisfaction than did on-campus learners.

Communication Preference. Communicating with students, regardless of the method of course delivery, can be challenging, at best. In the fourth section of the survey, students were asked how they prefer to receive initial information regarding programs and services, receive subsequent information, and how they prefer to send information. Results indicate that distance learners and on-campus learners overwhelmingly select e-mail as their preferred mode of communication, regardless of the type of information communicated. In addition, the two groups agree that the second most preferred mode of communication, for any type of information, is snail mail. The third most widely preferred mode of communication for both groups, for all types of information, was Web sites, with one exception. On-campus students selected the phone as their third choice of communication for sending information. The two groups split on their fourth choice. Distance education students preferred the phone for each type of information, while on-campus students preferred in-person contact as their fourth choice. Thus, when it comes to the phone versus in-person contact, distance education students prefer the phone and students on-campus prefer in-person, as would be expected.

Programs and Services. Units within and outside of student affairs provide programs and services to facilitate student learning. One of the primary goals of this study was to explore the importance of student services to distance learners compared to on-campus learners, regardless of where those services and programs administratively reside. Thus, the last section of the survey asked respondents to rate the importance of a collection of services and programs, as well as their satisfaction with each (see Table 4.2).

**Table 4.2. Programs and Services for Distance
and On-Campus Learners**

Program/Service	Importance		Satisfaction	
Service	DE	Campus	DE	Campus
Advising-Continuing Education Office	2.98	3.05	3.10	3.0*
Advising-Faculty	3.05	3.49**	3.05	2.97
Advising-Virtual Advising Center	2.56	2.58	3.07	3.04
Student ID	2.47	3.36**	3.07	3.28**
Bookstore	2.94	3.25**	3.13	2.98**
Career Center	2.47	3.04**	2.99	3.05
Cashiers Office	2.77	3.11**	3.04	2.97*
Chap Cooperative Ministry	2.01	2.34**	3.07	3.1
Computer Help Desk-College	2.67	2.94**	3.11	3.02*
Computer Help Desk-University	2.74	2.94**	3.08	3.03
Crafts Center	1.76	2.31**	3.18	3.0*
Dance	1.67	2.19**	3.11	2.93*
Dining	1.77	3.18**	2.98	2.75*
Financial Aid	2.63	3.48**	2.98	2.88
Gallery of Art and Design	1.82	2.51**	3.05	3.08
Greek Life	1.64	1.99**	3.03	2.73*
Health Promotion	2.08	3.03**	3.05	2.98
Housing	1.7	3.13**	2.97	2.79*
Libraries	3.03	3.62**	3.25	3.27
Multicultural Student Affairs	1.88	2.61**	3.00	3.00
Music	1.88	2.77**	3.01	2.93
OrientationContinuing Education	2.33	2.53**	3.02	2.99
Orientation-Degree Seeking	2.37	3.01**	2.92	2.89
Parents & Families Services	1.94	2.68**	2.94	2.97
Physical Education	2.05	3.02**	2.88	3.09**
Registration and Records	3.29	3.66**	3.13	3.19
Student Center	2.09	3.12**	2.96	3.06
Student Conduct	2.28	3.05**	2.98	2.96
Student Government	2.02	2.86**	2.86	2.76
Student Handbook	2.46	2.84**	3.00	2.96
Student Leadership	2.11	2.84**	2.97	3.04
Student Media	2.11	2.93**	3.05	2.98
Student Organizations	2.10	3.21**	3.02	3.13
Theater	1.94	2.68**	3.00	3.09
Women's Center	2.02	2.79**	3.08	3.15

*$p < .05$
**$p < .0001$

For services and programs currently available, many of the relationships between on-campus learners and distance learners were statistically significant with respect to both importance and satisfaction. However, the R-square values were extremely low for satisfaction and relatively low for importance, with the highest R-square value equaling .31. The highest R-square values were found between on-campus learners and distance learners in how they

Table 4.3. Likelihood of Distance Learners Using Programs and Services Currently Unavailable

Program/Service	Likely or Very Likely	Unlikely or Very Unlikely
Club Sports	14%	85%
Counseling Center	30%	71%
Fitness/Wellness	38%	62%
Gymnasium	44%	56%
Intramurals	15%	85%
Online Leadership Program	31%	68%
Outdoor Adventures	20%	80%
Student Health Services	32%	68%
Student Legal Services	28%	72%
Virtual Orientation	30%	70%

rated the importance of the following services: student center (.23), student organizations (.25), housing (.26), and dining (.31). The services rated highest in terms of importance to distance learners include registration and records, faculty advising, and libraries. In comparison, on-campus students rated registration and records, libraries, and student health services highest in terms of importance.

Distance learners at NC State University do not pay the majority of student fees and are therefore not eligible to participate in many student services provided to on-campus students. A primary goal of the survey was to determine if distance learners would indeed use selected student services if given the opportunity. Therefore, respondents were asked to rate how likely they were to use several student services for which they are currently ineligible (see Table 4.3).

In addition to examining how likely distance learners were to use these services and programs, they were also asked to rate the importance of each. In comparing their mean scores with those of on-campus learners, all of the relationships were statistically significant except for virtual orientation, which is not available to on-campus learners. However, the R-square values were relatively low, with the highest value for student health services at .28.

Implications

Several implications for practice emerged from the results of this study.

Programs and Services. Results from the survey indicated that while on-campus learners and distance learners do not differ tremendously in how satisfied they were with available services and programs, they do indeed differ in the importance they placed on these services and programs. As would be expected, the greatest differences were seen in services not traditionally utilized by distance learners, such as the student center, student organizations, housing, and dining. Instead, distance learners were more concerned with administrative services that are critical to their success, such as registration and records, advising, and the libraries. Perhaps they would place a higher value on other services and programs that are currently available to them if they were aware of these opportunities. Student affairs practitioners should be deliberate in marketing services and programs to this population.

Results of the survey also indicated that distance learners report they would likely use services and programs that are currently not at their disposal. For example, more than 30 percent of distance learners reported that they would likely or very likely use the counseling center, fitness or wellness facilities, gymnasium, online leadership development series, student health services, or virtual orientation, if they were available. These numbers are promising and should lead student affairs practitioners to delve more deeply into the possibility of offering such services and programs to this population.

The current profile of distance learners, along with previous studies and this study suggest that they desire only minimal transactional services. However, it is also clear that other services and programs would be welcome if available and are likely to be even more desirable to the new distance learner who chooses an online environment over a campus environment after high school. In addition, there are services and programs that may not be rated as important by distance learners and on-campus students alike, but that student affairs practitioners believe are critical to student development and learning. Many of these programs and services, such as leadership programs and support for marginalized groups, are not currently available to distance learners, but should be. Challenging the enrollment management-plus model is a key component to serving this growing and changing population successfully. Meeting this challenge requires educating other campus administrators about the role of student affairs and its contribution to student success. At NC State University, distance education administrators have embraced the notion of providing a broad spectrum of services and programs because of their belief that it is appropriate to do so and, pragmatically, because of the potential positive impact on retention.

Enrollment Growth and Changing Demographics. Student affairs administrators must stay abreast of institutional enrollment projections in order to anticipate the continued increase in the sheer number of distance learners as well as shifts in the demographic makeup of this population. Data from the Sloan Consortium (2004) predict large increases in online enrollments nationally with little evidence of a plateau at this time. The expected average growth rate is more than 20 percent, which far exceeds the rate of overall growth in the overall student body. The bottom line is that distance learners will represent a growing portion of the overall student population for some time. As fully developed degree programs are added to existing scattered course offerings, institutions can expect growth in the traditional distance education population, including older students who live at a distance and students sponsored by industry and the military.

Likewise, students who fit the traditional on-campus profile are increasingly interested in distance education opportunities as an alternative to traditional on-campus courses. In addition, students in the traditional range of eighteen to twenty-two years old will increasingly be exposed to precollege distance education offerings. The latest data from the U.S. Department of Education (Setzer and Lewis, 2005) indicate that 36 percent of public school districts had students enrolled in distance education courses in 2002–2003, and 72 percent of those districts plan to expand offerings in the future. Today's elementary school student may very well attend college directly after high school, but may also expect to receive much of that education in an on-line setting. The combination of shifting demographics and tremendous growth creates a considerable challenge for all of higher education.

Moreover, distance learners are a somewhat invisible population, which further increases the challenge to meet their needs. These students are not physically on campus and have limited in-person interaction with faculty, staff, and other students. Though there is an expected shift as more degree programs are developed, most of these students at NC State University are not matriculated into a degree program and enroll on a part-time basis. Distance learners, on the whole, are not given the same consideration as are on-campus students. Student affairs practitioners must carefully consider these three factors—enrollment growth, changing demographics, and invisibility—in serving this population.

Resources. There are significant resource implications for institutions and students in serving the distance learning population. First, providing services and programs from a distance requires maintaining pace with technological change, which requires a significant investment of resources. Second, institutions may need to impose student fees on distance learners that previously were not required in order to fund the provision of services and programs. Third, these efforts require significant administrative planning and partnerships within student affairs units and with other institutional service providers, especially the distance education administrative units.

At NC State University, the distance education administrative and student affairs units have partnered to improve the overall experience of distance learners and pitch distance education to new audiences. By proactively seeking to serve the distance learning population and seeking that partnership, student affairs administrators have an opportunity to bridge the widely acknowledged gap between student affairs and academic affairs (Kezar, Hirsch, and Burak, 2002). The benefits of a distance education partnership can spill over into other areas. NC State University's Division of Student Affairs actively participates in campuswide discussions, committees, and planning efforts as a result of the increased visibility achieved through partnerships with the distance education units.

Future Research. Given the explosion in distance education and the ongoing demographic shift of the distance learning population, researchers must continually assess the size of this population, the profile of the distance learner, and the needs of distance learners. In addition, researchers and practitioners must pay careful attention to another growing population, hybrid learners—those students who are taking both on-campus and distance education courses. All three populations—distance learners, on-campus learners, and hybrid learners—have special needs. Student affairs professionals, as well as other service professionals and researchers, must identify those needs and then provide appropriate services and programs. Future research should also explore the relationship between distance learner success and involvement in student services and programs. Similarly, researchers should explore the impact of distance on distance learners' use of and desire for services and programs: Do distance learners who live far away from campus want or need the same services as those who live in close proximity to the institution? Finally, researchers should examine administrative relationships between student affairs and distance education units and their impact on the academic success of distance learners.

Recommendations

As a result of this study, the following seven recommendations are offered to student affairs practitioners.

Student affairs administrators are encouraged to understand how distance education is administered at the institution and what current and projected enrollments are for the distance learning population.

Practitioners are encouraged to understand institutional definitions of distance education as well as the criteria for defining courses, degree programs, and students as "distance" and how these elements compare with the on-campus versions of each.

Student affairs administrators are encouraged to learn how distance education is funded at the institution and if those funds are available for providing services and programs to distance learners.

Student affairs administrators should be prepared to advocate for the role of student affairs in distance education at the institution and to educate others regarding the mission, objectives, administrative design, and leadership of the student affairs unit and units within it.

Student fees must be given careful consideration as they apply to distance learners. Any fees imposed on distance learners should be adequate to fund the respective services or programs. Likewise, distance learners should receive equitable services and programs for any fees paid. This may seem to be an obvious point, but it is worth considering when the students involved are generally at such a distance that the provision of existing services and programs is very difficult.

While some existing programs and services initially developed for on-campus students can be adapted for distance learners, new programs

and services may need to be developed to meet any special needs of this population.
Chief student affairs officers are encouraged to assign leadership duties associated with serving the distance learning population. Such delegation can be accomplished by establishing a position dedicated solely to these activities, by these activities constituting one designated duty of a position, through a committee, or through a combination of these approaches.
Regardless of which method is used, formalizing a commitment to serving this population will increase the likelihood of success.

Conclusion

At NC State University, this survey project has moved the institution forward in its efforts to serve the distance learning population. Within the Division of Student Affairs, departments now have a better understanding of the needs and interests of distance learners and are actively seeking enrollment planning information as they retrofit existing programs and services and develop new ones for this population. A campuswide effort to address changes in the student fee structure is underway, and student service providers will consider the survey data in the decision-making process. Administrators in the university's technology and distance education units have a better understanding of the distance learning population and of the role of the Division of Student Affairs.

Student affairs practitioners are committed to serving all students, regardless of any factor that differentiates them from the mainstream. As a profession, student affairs must now recognize that students who choose to learn from a distance are part of the institutional community and should be provided equitable resources, services, and programs. The challenges of understanding and serving the distance learning population are significant. Creating formal partnerships between student affairs and the distance education administration is a critical component in overcoming those challenges. Closing this gap will result in strengthening the triangular relationship between technology, distance education, and student affairs and will help move our institutions toward a more inclusive model.

References

Beaudoin, M. F. "Distance Education Leadership for a New Century." *Online Journal of Distance Learning Administration*, 2003, 6(2)." http://www.westga.edu/%7Edistance/ojdla/summer62/beaudoin62.html. Accessed May 10, 2005.

Blimling, G. S., and Whitt, E. J. *Good Practice in Student Affairs: Principles to Foster Student Learning*. San Francisco: Jossey-Bass, 1999.

Connick, G. P. "Student Services for Distance Learners." *NetResults*. 2001. http://www.naspa.org/membership/mem/nr/article.cfm?id=208. Accessed May 31, 2005.

Council of Regional Accrediting Commissions. "Statement of Commitment by the Regional Accrediting Commissions for the Evaluation of Electronically Offered Degree and Certificate Programs." 2001. http://www.wascweb.org/senior/Statement_of_ Commitment.pdf. Accessed May 31, 2005.

Dirr, P. J. *Putting Principles into Practice: Promoting Effective Support Services for Students in Distance Learning Programs: A Report on Findings of a Survey.* Alexandria, Va.: Public Service Telecommunications Corporation, 1999.

Floyd, D., and Casey-Powell, D. "New Roles for Student Support Services in Distance Learning." In B. L. Bowler and K. P. Hardy (eds.), *From Distance Education to E-Learning: Lessons Along the Way.* New Directions for Community Colleges, no. 128. San Francisco: Jossey-Bass, 2004.

Hirt, J. B., Cain, D., Bryant, B., and Williams, E. "Cyberservices: What's Important and How Are We Doing." *NASPA Journal,* 2003, *40*(2), 98–118.

Howell, S. L., Williams, P. B., and Lindsay, N. K. "Thirty-Two Trends Affecting Distance Education: An Informed Foundation for Strategic Planning." *Online Journal of Distance Learning Administration,* 2003, *6*(3). http://www.westga.edu/~distance/ojdla/fall63/howell63.html. Accessed May 31, 2005.

Husmann, D. E., and Miller, M. T. "Improving Distance Education: Perceptions of Program Administrators." *Online Journal of Distance Learning Administration,* 2001, *4*(1). http://www.westga.edu/~distance/ojdla/spring41/husmann41.html. Accessed May 31, 2005.

Kezar, A., Hirsch, D. J., and Burak, C. (eds.). *Understanding the Role of Academic and Student Affairs Collaboration in Creating a Successful Learning Environment.* San Francisco: Jossey-Bass, 2002.

Krauth, B., and Carbajal, J. *Guide to Developing Online Student Services.* Boulder, Colo.: Western Cooperative for Educational Telecommunications (WCET), 1999.

Kretovics, M. "The Role of Student Affairs in Distance Education: Cyber-Services or Virtual Communities." *Online Journal of Distance Learning Administration,* 2003, *6*(3). http://www.westga.edu/~distance/ojdla/fall63/kretovics63.html. Accessed May 31, 2005.

LaPadula, M. "A Comprehensive Look at Online Student Support Services for Distance Learners." *American Journal of Distance Education,* 2003, *7*(2), 119–128.

Levy, S. "Six Factors to Consider When Planning Online Distance Learning Programs in Higher Education." *Online Journal of Distance Learning Administration,* 2003, *6*(1). http://www.westga.edu/%7Edistance/ojdla/spring61/levy61.htm. Accessed May 31, 2005.

Levy, S., and Beaulieu, R. "Online Distance Learning Among the California Community Colleges: Looking at the Planning and Implementation." *American Journal of Distance Education,* 2003, *17*(4), 207–220.

McClendon E., and Cronk, P. "Rethinking Academic Management Practices: A Case of Meeting New Challenges in Online Delivery." *Online Journal of Distance Learning Administration,* 1999, *2*(1). http://www.westga.edu/~distance/mclendon21.html. Accessed May 31, 2005.

Meyers, P., and Ostash, H. "Pulling the Pieces Together: Comprehensive Online Support Services." *IJournal—Insight into Student Services, 2004,* Issue 8. http://www.ijournal.us/issue_08/ij_issue08_MeyersAndOstash_01.htm. Accessed May 31, 2005.

Moe, M. T. "Emerging Trends in Post-Secondary Education: The View to 2012." Paper presented at the conference, "Driving Post-Secondary Education," by Education Industry Finance and Investment Summit, 2002. http://www.usdla.org/ppt/THINKEQUITY.ppt. Accessed May 31, 2005.

Nesbitt, J. *Megatrends: Ten New Directions Transforming Our Lives.* New York: Warner, 1982.

North Carolina State University. *2015 Draft Enrollment Plan.* Raleigh, N.C.: State University, 2005.

Pascarella, E. T., and Terenzini, P. T. *How College Affects Students.* San Francisco: Jossey-Bass, 1991.

Peters, O. *Learning and Teaching in Distance Education: Analyses and Interpretations from an International Perspective.* London: Kogan Page, 1998.

Rinear, K. "How to Deliver Integrated Support to Your Students." *Distance Education Report,* 2003, 7(2), 3–6.

Setzer, J. C., and Lewis, L. *Distance Education Courses for Public Elementary and Secondary School Students: 2002–03.* (NCES 2005–010). Washington, D.C.: National Center for Education Statistics, 2005.

Sloan Consortium. *Entering the Mainstream: The Quality and Extent of Online Education in the United States, 2003 and 2004.* Needham, Mass.: Alfred P. Sloan Foundation.

Southern Association of Colleges and Schools. "Best Practices for Electronically Offered Degree and Certificate Programs." 2000. http://www.sacscoc.org/pdf/commadap.pdf. Accessed May 31, 2005.

Twigg, C. A., and Oblinger, D. G. The Virtual University. A Report from a Joint Educom/IBM Roundtable. Washington, D.C.: Educom, 1996.

Visser, L., and Visser, Y. L. "Perceived and Actual Student Support Needs in Distance Education." *Quarterly Review of Distance Education,* 2000, 1(2), 109–117.

Western Cooperative for Educational Telecommunications (WCET). "Beyond the Administrative Core: Creating Web-Based Student Services for Online Learners." 2003. http://www.wcet.info/projects/laap. Accessed May 31, 2005.

LESLIE A. DARE *is director of distance education and technology services for the division of student affairs at North Carolina State University.*

LISA P. ZAPATA *is assistant vice chancellor for student affairs at North Carolina State University.*

AMANDA G. THOMAS *is a doctoral student in higher education administration at North Carolina State University.*

5

Providing high-quality student services to students enrolled in distance education programs is a critical link to the academic success of this growing student population.

Implementing the Web of Student Services

Janet Ross Kendall

While on-campus student affairs offices have recognized for years that good student services are essential for students' success, applying that attitude toward students off campus has emerged more recently. Over the past few years, providing quality student services to distance students has been a hot topic in books and journals and at conferences. Institutions are recognizing that support services for distance students are essential if those students are to be as successful as on-campus students. Further, as students experience high-tech and high-quality services from online providers such as Amazon and Zappos, schools recognize they need to work hard to improve their Web sites, their attitudes, and the services they provide.

Much of the interest in providing quality services to distance students has been the result of a project undertaken between 2000 and 2002 by the Western Cooperative for Educational Telecommunications (WCET) called "Creating Web-Based Student Services for Online Learners." This project was funded by the U.S. Department of Education and its Fund for the Improvement of Postsecondary Education (FIPSE) through the Learning Anytime Anyplace Partnership (LAAP) and resulted in the development of guidelines for institutions to use when putting their student services online (Western Cooperative for Educational Telecommunications, 2003).

One very valuable outcome of the WCET project was the creation of a graphic, "Web of Student Services," that displays the various student services recommended for online learners (see Figure 2.1 in Chapter Two).

The web specifies services in five categories that are to be provided in an integrated rather than isolated way: academic services suite, personal services suite, student communities suite, communications suite, and the administrative core. We have used this as a model for the services our staff developed at Washington State University (WSU) for students enrolled through Distance Degree Programs (DDP).

Washington State University's Distance Degree Programs

WSU offers distance bachelor's degrees in six undergraduate fields—social sciences, humanities, criminal justice, business administration, human development, and nursing—through its Distance Degree Programs (DDP). The program began in 1992 with fifty-seven students and now has approximately 5,500 enrollments each semester; more than 1,400 students have graduated with their bachelor's degrees. From the beginning, we recognized that quality student services were equally as important for student success as quality academic programs and worked hard to provide both. We made sure that all policies applied equally to distance and on-campus students; when they didn't, we worked with the administrative units to draft new policies and had them approved by the Faculty Senate. For each service we planned to provide for distance students, we collaborated closely with the on-campus unit that offered that service so that the service that distance students received was similar to that available to on-campus students (such as financial aid, career counseling, and the online writing lab) and, equally important, that the on-campus unit participated in the development and provision of that service and thus was committed to it. When the on-campus unit was unable to make the service available to distance students we investigated, with that unit's support, other ways of providing the service. As one example, we outsourced tutoring to Smarthinking.com when the campus student center was unable to expand its services to meet this need.

The remainder of this article focuses on how services are provided to students enrolled at WSU to obtain their bachelor's degrees through DDP. In addition, it gives examples of exemplary distance student services provided by other institutions. The WCET web categories are used as organizers for the discussions of these services.

Administrative Core and the Academic Services Suite Provided Through *My DDP*

My DDP is a sophisticated Web portal we have developed (written in Visual FoxPro 6.0) that allows us to provide customized, exemplary student services. The portal allows students to access information about their distance courses, to update information, submit course work, nominate proctors or request exams, and submit evaluations, as well as providing links to other resources. Students log in to My DDP with their university network ID and password. Once logged in, the My DDP Student Menu appears (see Figure 5.1).

Figure 5.1. My DDP Student Menu

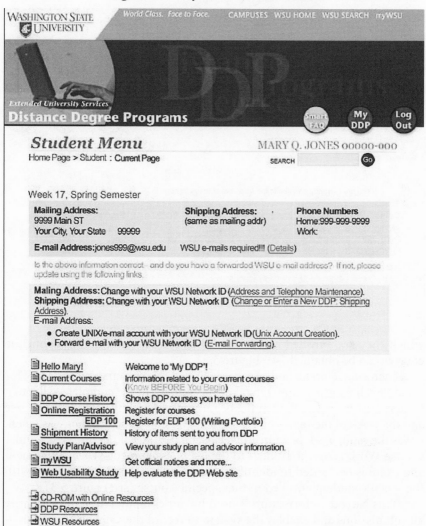

Students are prompted to update their contact information through various links and are welcomed to My DDP. They can view their course history, register for the required university Writing Portfolio exam, access advising information, and view items sent to them from DDP since they began taking courses (Shipment History). There is also a link to *MyWSU*, which is where official university notices are displayed. Finally, there are links to various resources students might find helpful.

Viewing Course Information. Once students are familiar with My DDP, they usually go directly into Current Courses, where the courses in

Figure 5.2. My DDP Current Courses

Course	Cr.	Begin	End	Week	Course Work	Shipment Tracking	Provide Feedback	Login
ANTH 499	0	8/24/04	12/10/04	10	view		enter	n/a
ENGL 389	3	8/23/04	12/10/04	10	view	view	enter	Web CT
PSYCH 333	3	1/11/05	4/29/05	10	view		enter	n/a

• **Completed Courses:** Completed courses will stay on this page for 21 days after the completed date. Course Work will not be viewable after that time.

which they are enrolled are listed and additional information about the courses can be obtained (see Figure 5.2).

Each course prefix and number is linked to the course syllabus (so, for example, clicking on Engl 355 takes the student to the complete syllabus). Course credits are listed, then the beginning and ending dates of the course and the week of the semester are shown. (When this screenshot was taken, it was the tenth week of a fifteen-week semester.) Clicking on "view" under Course Work takes the student to the list of assignments; each assignment and exam is bar-coded to identify the particular assignment or exam with the specific student enrolled in that specific course (see Figure 5.3).

This barcode information is used by our computer system to identify all submissions and enables the system to record the date when an assignment was received and processed (in the example, 10/25/2004), along with the date the instructor returned the graded assignment (10/29/2004) and the grade that was assigned. Students can also request to have an exam sent to their proctor; clicking on the "Request" link brings up a Proctor Nomination Form that the student completes and submits to our office; we then send the exam to the nominated proctor. The date it was sent is then shown, and if the student clicks on the date, the name and address of the proctor to whom it was sent are displayed. Once the student takes the exam and the proctor sends it to us, the date our office processed it and sent it to the instructor and the date the instructor returned it, along with the grade, are shown.

Figure 5.3. My DDP List of Assignments

WASHINGTON STATE
UNIVERSITY

World Class. Face to Face.   CAMPUSES   WSU HOME   WSU SEARCH   myWSU

Extended University Services
Distance Degree Programs

Smart FAQ   My DDP   Log Out

ENGL 389   MARY Q. JONES 00000-000
Home Page > Student : Current Page   SEARCH   Go

Course Work

Please review Instructions

Instructor(s): John T. Smith

Description	Processed	Returned	Exam Sent	Grade	Barcode
Literary Analysis	9/20/2004	9/27/2004			2908081
Midterm Examination	10/25/2004	10/29/2004	10/13/2004	B	2908082
Midterm Examination 2					2908083
Final Evaluation	12/20/2004	12/20/2004	Request		2908084

Back on the Current Courses page (Figure 5.2), the student can click on "view" under Shipment Tracking to see information about her course materials (see Figure 5.4) what materials were shipped, the fee charged, the date they were requested and shipped, and the address to which they were shipped (available by clicking "view" under Address).

Another link on the Current Courses page allows the student to provide feedback to our office as they are working through the course, and, if the course is in an online learning space (for example, Web CT), there is a link to that space.

When the student is finished with the next-to-last assignment for a course, the Online Evaluation link is automatically displayed at the bottom of the course work listing (Figure 5.3). Instructors also send out notices to their students encouraging them to complete these evaluations. A link to the DDP survey is also generated by the system.

Other Services Within the Administrative Core. All services within the administrative core are provided by central WSU offices, although DDP does provide certain information on its Web site. As previously noted, since distance programs were approved in 1992, we have ensured that all policies and procedures apply equally to distance and on-campus students. Now, if you go to the WSU Admissions Web site, DDP is included under the Undergraduate category (see Figure 5.5).

Counselors in the Office of Financial Aid and Scholarship Services have all been trained to answer basic questions about aid for distance students;

Figure 5.4. My DDP Shipment Tracking

more in-depth questions go to a counselor who specializes in aid for distance and branch-campus students. Students' accounts and records are held centrally, and as of fall 2004, all WSU students can register for all classes at all locations through one central system. Class schedules and catalogs are also held centrally; in addition, information about DDP classes is also displayed through the DDP Website (distance.wsu.edu/courses).

The Web sites of every university serving distance students that we have reviewed include links to the elements included on the WCET Administrative Core. For example, Penn State Online has a searchable course catalog (http://www.worldcampus.psu.edu/search/index.shtml), and details about financial aid available to distance students are included on the main Penn State financial aid Web site (http//:www.psu.edu/studentaid/aidprog/disted.html). The Texas Telecampus provides a link directly from

Figure 5.5. WSU Admissions Application

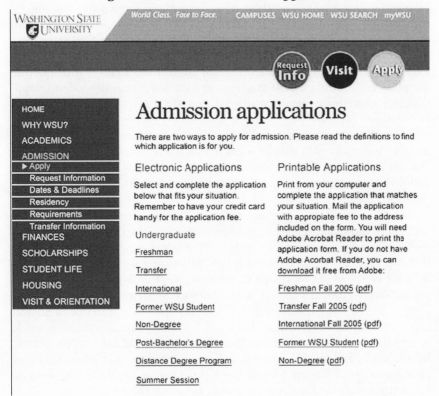

its home page to its registration pages (http://telecampus.utsystem.edu/index.cfm/4,0,76,61,html); this page encourages both degree-seeking and non-degree-seeking students to download registration checklists, and it provides links to the academic calendar and student handbook.

Academic Services Suite

In addition to services described in the previous sections about My DDP, professional advisors have been part of the DDP staff since the beginning to provide academic advising and counseling for distance learners. The advisers have worked very closely with their counterparts in the academic departments to ensure that they are following the same procedures and guidelines as on-campus advisers. There was some controversy early on as to whether the on-campus advisers should work with distance students. That was quickly dispelled when on-campus advisers recognized that it is more efficient for advisers who aren't pulled in several directions to work with distance students—on-campus advisers were finding they were playing the ultimate game of phone tag with distance students because their on-campus responsibilities kept taking them away from their phones and computers. Further, on-campus advisers recognized they were unprepared to deal with the myriad support services distance students needed.

DDP advisors have developed several systems that help them provide excellent service to their students. Each advisor has a clever introduction for prospective and current students to view via streaming video (http://distance.wsu.edu/prospective/adv_info.asp#DDPAdvised). Through their personalized My DDP page, current students are directed to advising pages, where information from their adviser is posted, and they can download their most recent study plan that advisers update each semester. The study plan lists each student's degree requirements, how the courses they have taken fulfill those requirements, and what they need to take to complete their degrees.

Having DDP staff provide technical support to distance students seemed to duplicate services the university's Student Computing Services (SCS) could provide. Consequently, DPP worked closely with SCS staff to develop procedures they would follow in helping distance students. Rio Salado College of the Maricopa Community College System provides comprehensive technical support to its distance students. Their home page states, "Rio Salado's Instructional Support Helpdesk is available to answer questions about your course, help you contact your instructor, provide Successful Start [an orientation that previews their eLearning programs] information, and to help you work through instructional issues that may arise during your 'Online Experience'." (http://www.riosalado.edu/services/student/support/helpdesk/instructional_helpdesk.shtml).

Because Portland Community College's online distance learning courses are provided in the WebCT learning environment, their technical support page is called "WebCT@PCC," and it provides links to a variety of topics as well as a phone number and e-mail address to the Student Help Desk (https://webct.pcc.edu/support/).

For many years Washington State University's bookstore sold textbooks to distance students who called on a toll-free line. However, DDP staff worked with a local copy center to make copies of course guides, which we mailed out as students registered in each course. We recognized the amount of staff time we were spending on this, so we successfully negotiated with the bookstore to assume this task. Students can now order all textbooks and materials through the bookstore's online site, which has a special link to DDP texts (http://www.wsubookie.net/ddpfaq.html). Most distance learning programs provide access for students to online textbook ordering. The University of Georgia provides textbooks through MBS Direct (http://www.gactr.uga.edu/idl/courses/textbooks.phtml). In contrast, textbooks for distance learning courses offered through Kansas State University are available at Varney's Bookstore, the university's local bookstore,(http://www.dce.ksu.edu/dce/division/studenthandbook/textbooks/index.html).

Florida State University combines textbooks, study guides, and media needed for online courses into a "Course Packet," which is available at both the university bookstore and another local bookstore (http://online.fsu. edu/student/degree/attend/order/).

As DDP developed media to go with our courses, we also needed assistance in mailing the videotapes and CDs to students. Our university shipping unit performed similar duties, so we talked with staff about taking over the mailing of our materials; the DPP program now funds a half-time staff person there whose computer is networked with our office so that shipping labels are generated as students register. Each item is bar-coded, and, as explained earlier, as each item is shipped that barcode is associated with a particular student. The student can click on the barcode, and when the material is returned, staff scan the barcode so the system knows that she has returned her materials and will not be charged a non-return penalty fee.

WSU's Libraries Director recognized the importance of providing reference services to distance students, and a librarian responsible for responding to the needs of distance students has been part of the library staff since the program began. Libraries' staff developed a class on library use that they modified to serve both on- and off-campus students; staff have also developed Distance Degree Library Services Web pages for distance students. Over the years we have worked with the Libraries to fine-tune their processes for serving distance students; as on-campus students search the Libraries' electronic catalog and databases from their dorm rooms, staff are finding that they are applying some of the procedures they developed for off-campus students to on-campus students. Other institutions also provide library services for their distance students. For example, the University of Alabama has a Web page for distance learning students that provides links to a variety of services they might need (http://www.lib.ua.edu/distanceed/), including an "Ask a Librarian" option, a "Subject Guides" link that allows students to browse pages developed by subject-matter librarians, and a link that provides instructions for requesting materials. The University of Houston also has a page devoted to library services for distance students (http://info.lib.uh.edu /services/distance.html) that explains how students who are taking some or all of their courses at a distance can access information and materials.

Students may need tutoring services as they progress toward their degree. Assistance with writing papers is provided by the Online Writing Lab (OWL), to which any WSU student has access. We have worked with OWL staff to ensure that distance students are well served. However, we were unsuccessful in trying to broaden students' access to other WSU tutoring services so, as mentioned, we outsourced that service to Smarthinking. com. Weber State University's tutoring system is particularly noteworthy; it has developed its own tutoring system for distance students (http:// weber.edu/tutoringservices.xml) and provides one-on-one learning assistance by Weber State students, who receive tutoring training certified by the College Reading and Learning Association (see Figure 5.6).

Figure 5.6. Weber State Tutoring Services

Tutoring Services

Welcome to the Tutoring Services Web Site. Please take time to browse the site (using the links on the left), and e-mail us with any comments you have that will assist in making this site more helpful: tutoring@weber.edu.

Mission Statement

Tutoring services supports the mission of Weber State University and the Student Services Division by providing quality, **one-on-one learning assistance** by certified tutors who encourage and guide students in the development of their potential as independent learners.

Staff Information

The Tutoring Services tutors are WSU students who have successufly completed the course(s) they tutor and instructors have recommended many. All tutors receive training in tutoring skills by attending a credit training course nationally certified by the College Reading and Learning Association (CRLA).

Please Note: Summer tutoring will be availiable on a limited basis beginning May 16.

Additonal Help

On-Line Math Tutoring

Drop-In Math Tutoring

Natural Science Learning Center Drop-In Tutoring

Social Science Learning Center Drop-In Tutoring

Skills Enhancement Center

Supplemental Instruction

Writing Center

West Center Drop-In Tutoring

Academic Support Tutoring at Davis

Study Skills

Providing accommodations for students with disabilities is coordinated through WSU's Disability Resource Center (DRC). The same procedures are followed when distance students request accommodations as those required for on-campus students. A DDP staff member is the liaison to the DRC and works with distance students to provide documentation of their disability. That staff member also assists other DDP staff in providing the appropriate accommodations (such as extra time for testing, transcripts of audio materials). Other institutions with Web pages describing services to distance students with disabilities include the Open University of the United Kingdom (http://www.open.ac.uk/disability/) and the Penn State World Campus (http://www.worldcampus.psu.edu/wc/StudentServices_StudentsDisabilities.shtml).

Communications Suite

WSU contracts with RightNow Technologies to host a SmartFAQ site, linked directly from our home page, where visitors to our Web site can search for answers to a wide variety of questions. The My DDP sites for students and faculty provide means for communication among faculty, students, staff, and the institution. To further promote a connection with DDP, staff photos are posted on our staff Web site page (distance.wsu.edu/about/staff.asp). We also send out a monthly e-mail to all students reminding them of deadlines and providing various types of information, and we mail out newsletters once each semester. (Monthly e-mail announcements and newsletters are at distance.wsu.edu/resources/anncmnts/anncmnt-index.asp and distance. wsu.edu/pubs/index.asp#news.) We host an Open House on the WSU Pullman campus each fall, another event on the west side of the state each spring, and two graduation receptions each year, one for December and one for May graduation. Advisors and other staff also make trips to the various WSU Learning Centers around the state (learningcenters.wsu.edu) in order to encourage communication with students.

Other institutions provide information to students in a variety of ways. The Oregon State University eCampus has an eCampus Knowledge Base that allows students to access answers to questions in the database (http:// ecampus.oregonstate.edu/ask-ecampus/knowledge-base/default.htm). They also schedule Live Chats with their staff and invite "Guest Hosts," such as a career services representative (http://ecampus.oregonstate.edu/chat/host/ default.htm) (see Figure 5.7).

The UT Telecampus has won awards for its online newsletter, *UT4ME* (http://www.telecampus.utsystem.edu/index.cfm/4,1224,html). Eastern Oregon University publishes a monthly online newsletter, *DDEzine*, (http:// www.eou.edu/dde/DDEzine/DDEzine.htm), which includes articles about library support, reminds students about important policies, and provides hotlinks to numerous student support sites; students can also access archives of previous issues. Weber State University provides a lengthy list of FAQs to assist students in finding information about a variety of topics (http://wsuonline.weber.edu/students/faq/).

Student Communities Suite

WSU has worked hard to develop student activities for distance students and is one of the few traditional institutions that has a student government specifically for that group of students (http://www.aswsu-ddp.wsu.edu/). Students conduct business in senate meetings every two weeks in an online chat room, campaign for office, and contribute through a number of senate committees.

WSU also has two activities in which students can be involved to help other students in their courses. Students in the last couple of semesters of their programs, or those who have already graduated, can volunteer to be mentors of new students (http://www.aswsu-ddp.wsu.edu/mentor/). Some courses have Virtual Facilitators who help students enrolled in courses to use the tools in the online environment as effectively as possible to create what we call an "active class community" (http://distance.wsu.edu/pubs/

Figure 5.7. Oregon State Live Chat

Live Chat

Chat Now | Meet Our Hosts | Help

Welcome to Ecampus Live Chat. This is an interactive session where you can submit questions and comments to our staff and guest hosts. Please review the Live Chat Schedule below to find the chats you would like to participate in. Before entering a chat, here is a quick review of what you need to know to get started.

- **"Prefered Chat Name"**- This is the name you choose to use during chats. It will appear during the session when you ask questions and make comments.
- **"Select a room"**- A host must be present in a room before you can enter. In addition, there may be more than one chat occuring at a time, so you need to select which chat you want to go to.
- **"Policy"**- You will be asked to read the policy before you can start.

Go to Live Chat Now

Live Chat Schedule (Pacific Standard Time)

Week: May 16-May 20, 2005	Time	Topic	Host
Monday	9am-10am	Student Services & General Information	Brett
Tuesday			
Wednesday	3pm-4pm	Student Services & General Information	Brett
Thursday	10am-11am	Student Services & General Information	Brett
	12pm	Guest Hosts-Leslie Soriano, Career Services	Leslie
	2pm-3pm	Enrollment & Degree Programs	Kay
Friday	11am-12pm	Student Services & General Information	
	3pm-4pm	Enrollment & Degree Programs	

newsletter/back/n03–2.pdf). The University of Maryland University College also provides mentoring opportunities for its students as part of the Career and Cooperative Education Center, with a link to "Find a Mentor/Be a Mentor," explaining "The best way to decide on a new career is to talk to someone who knows what it's like, day in and day out" (http://umuc.edu/careercenter/stu_find.html).

Some universities that serve distance learners have a special section of the Web pages for certain student population segments. For example, Penn State has extensive information for military students (http://www.world campus.psu.edu/wc/StudentServices_Military.shtml), including specific information on "How to Get Started" and "Credit for Military Experience." Few institutions focus on distance learning students as part of their alumni association. The University of Maryland University College is one exception, with a link for alumni directly from its home page (http://umuc.edu/alum/alum.html).

Personal Services Suite

Of the seven services listed under the Personal Services Suite, many universities serving distance students provide orientation. Eastern Oregon University offers an extensive distance education orientation, using the metaphor of a trek through their academic offerings and policies (http://www.eou.edu/dde/orient/orient.html). Portland Community College also has a comprehensive online orientation (http://www.distance.pcc.edu/orientation/mod1/mod1_succ.cfm) that compares the online and classroom environments; discusses skills of successful online students; offers two quizzes, one with "preliminary questions to ask yourself to see if you and online learning are a good match" and the second to evaluate students' technical skills; and provides detailed information about WebCT navigation.

Career services are also available at many schools serving distance learners. Weber State University offers a Virtual Career Center (http://departments.weber.edu/careerservices/) that serves students, faculty, alumni, and employers. Oregon State University's eCampus links to the campus Career Services office, which "provides opportunities to develop skills and knowledge for career and life-planning. Distance students are invited to participate in career counseling, mock interviews, and real interviews by phone or videoconference" (http://ecampus.oregonstate.edu/services/student-services/career_services.htm). The WSU student government funds a career counselor who provides various services, including a one-credit course on career planning for distance students (http://www.careers.wsu.edu/content/DDP/CareerClass.html).

A few schools offer placement services for students. University of Maryland University College offers "Career Quest," where students and alumni can post their resumes for local and national employers to review (http://www.umuc.edu/careercenter/stu_register.html).

Personal counseling for distance students seems to be available only rarely, for obvious reasons. WSU includes the following statement on its counseling services Web site: "Although direct counseling for DDP students cannot be provided, including by e-mail or telephone, assistance in finding local resources may be facilitated. Students with special referral questions or needs may consult by telephone with professional staff at Counseling Services," and provides the phone and office hours (http://www.counsel.wsu.edu/).

Conclusion

The importance of providing quality services to students studying at a distance cannot be overemphasized. The WCET student services web provides an excellent configuration of the array of services institutions can and, in most cases, should make available to online learners. The examples provided in this chapter demonstrate the variety of ways that distance learning programs can support students taking their courses. Programs can collaborate with units on their campuses that already make services available to on-campus students (such as disability services and library services), they can outsource to established providers (for example, tutoring services), or they can develop their own processes and procedures (such as for advising and orientations).

Reference

Western Cooperative for Educational Telecommunications (WCET). "Beyond the Administrative Core: Creating Web-Based Student Services for Online Learners." 2003. http://www.wcet.info/projects/laap/guidelines/overview.asp. Accessed May 8, 2005.

JANET ROSS KENDALL is director of distance degree programs at Washington State University.

6

Electronic portfolios are becoming more prevalent on colleges and universities and can be a valuable tool in assessment efforts on campus.

Electronic Co-Curricular Student Portfolios—Putting Them into Practice

Marilee J. Bresciani

Assessment of student learning and development is not new to student affairs professionals. The authors of the Student Learning Imperative (ACPA, 1996) have illustrated student affairs professionals' role in learning prior to 1994. It seems more recent however, that accreditors and other constituents are demanding evidence of how everyone in higher education is contributing to student learning. Moreover, conversations such as those reported in the Association of American Colleges and Universities' (AAC&U) report, *Greater Expectations: A New Vision for Learning as a Nation Goes to College* (AAC&U, 2003) are calling for all to enter into conversations about shared institutional learning goals.

The first step to contributing to a discussion about institutional student learning principles is that everyone articulate what is valuable related to student learning, including student affairs. The further clarification of how those values are delivered and evaluated through outcomes assessment is the next key step in grasping the values that many administrators and faculty have in common. Through student affairs assessment of student learning, evidence of contributions to shared values such as ethics, problem solving, and diversity can arise. Through assessment, the door to institutional competency conversations can open—for everyone. This chapter illustrates one method that can help faculty and co-curricular professionals come together to evaluate shared learning outcomes or common institutional learning principles.

An Overview of Outcomes Assessment

Outcomes assessment is a systematic, iterative process that allows faculty and co-curricular specialists to reflect on and communicate the intended results of their work. Through reflection of the learning that faculty and co-curricular specialists value (mission and goals), the articulation of what the end results of the learning will look like (outcome), and through the careful planning of the delivery of the learning and gathering of evidence (program planning and implementation, data gathering, analysis, interpretation of findings), assessment provides faculty and co-curricular specialists with the means to communicate what has been occurring in the curricular and co-curricular programs and the resources needed to ensure that the learning meets expectations for it (making decisions and recommendations based on the assessment findings).

Simply put, assessment allows program coordinators to answer the following questions on a continuous basis:

• What are we trying to do and why? Or, What is my program supposed to accomplish (outcomes)?
• How well are we doing it?
• How do we know?
• How do we use the information to improve our program or celebrate successes?
• Do we follow up later to see that the decisions we made are actually improving the program? (Bresciani, 2002)

Often these questions are posed to programs and answered by them in a vacuum. In other words, a program whose faculty teaches students how to become political scientists answers these questions for themselves, while another program that teaches students about leadership skills answers these questions for themselves. Certainly, reflecting on these questions and answering them is a positive and productive way to improve a program. Yet, without communication with other programs about what is being learned through these assessment efforts, the challenges posed by the AAC&U's *Greater Expectations* report *to* bring the unique work of each program together to articulate shared learning outcomes and provide the means for each evaluation will remain unanswered.

There are several ways in which one can progress in this conversation about shared learning outcomes; this article highlights the use of electronic student portfolios to manage such a conversation.

Definition of Portfolios

Portfolios are "a type of assessment in which students' work is systematically collected and carefully reviewed for evidence of learning and development" (Palomba and Banta, 1999, p. 131). Often, portfolios are constructed in order to ask students to reflect on their own learning (Alverno College, 2001) as well as to provide evidence of their learning to others. Kruger (2003) describes many uses of portfolios for student affairs professionals in his article, "Electronic Portfolios: The Next Big Thing?"

Portfolios can be used to evaluate student learning at the institutional or college level, or at the division, program, workshop, course, or individual student learning level. As such, portfolios can be used to link outcomes and resulting evidence and decisions from one program to another. Huba and Freed (2000) illustrate such a portfolio in which the student and co-curricular specialist evaluate a single outcome or set of outcomes related to each other. The examples in this article are based on the Huba and Freed portfolio type.

Articulating Outcomes

Prior to exploring the use of an electronic student portfolio in the context of Huba and Freed's model, the program must first have taken the time to define what it wants the end results of its program to be or the intended end results of the planned delivery of student learning and development. In other words, program leaders must have first articulated the program's student learning and development outcomes.

Using a student leadership program as an example, some of the intended results of the two-year co-curricular program, which primarily consists of workshops, retreats, and field experiences, include the following outcomes:

- Students will be able to debate accurately and clearly varying points of views of a selected topic.
- Students will be able to identify ethical dilemmas among various leadership scenarios.
- Students will be able to articulate their Myers-Briggs personality type and evaluate the impact of the type's tendencies on their organizational skills.
- Students will be able to identify problems and propose solutions in various organizational behavior case studies.

Some outcomes from a four-year political science academic program might include the following:

- Students will be able to apply their viewpoints effectively, efficiently, and persuasively in both writing and speaking to issues of public policy.
- Students will be able to collaborate effectively on group projects.
- Students will organize their internship portfolio of learning artifacts in a manner that relates to their career or advanced educational goals.
- Students will be able to identify ethical dilemmas that may come about when drafting public policies.

Examining these outcomes, one can see some shared values begin to emerge: writing and speaking, organizational skills, problem solving, analytical and critical thinking, and ethical reasoning. There are values present in one program that may also be in another, yet not yet articulated, such as collaboration and the ability to work in groups.

If these programs are provided with a way to map their program outcomes to institutional values, the clarity of how each program—whether it is curricular or co-curricular—contributes to the shared learning principles becomes more evident. Where institutions have not yet articulated these shared learning values, such common values can emerge from a document analysis of the assessment plans themselves.

An electronic portfolio that allows for the documentation of program outcomes enables each student to be aware of the intended outcomes for every program in which the student participates. In addition, it helps the student, the program, and the institution better understand the intended learning that is taking place and how the learning relates from program to program and student to student.

Implementation

After having articulated the student learning and development outcomes for each program, the program leaders need to understand how they will deliver the intended end results and how they will gather the information to evaluate the intended learning. Often, use of concept maps (Bresciani, 2003) can help the program identify the best ways to deliver the outcomes and the naturally occurring ways in which to evaluate them (Ewell, 2003). (For more details about concept mapping, see http://www.naspa.org/membership/mem/nr/article.cfm?id=1291.)

The important point is that the way in which the student learning is delivered and the way in which it is evaluated need to make sense to those who are doing the teaching and those who are learning. In other words, a political scientist may teach and evaluate ethical reasoning differently from a student leadership co-curricular specialist. That is not a problem. In fact, if the teachers are forced to use the same method, the potentially rich learning experience for each student may be hampered. At the very least, the instructor may lose out on the applicability of the results of the evidence and how to use it to improve the learning that was intended. In addition, the student may miss out on the richness of the transference and applicability of ethical reasoning of political scientists to student organizational leaders. An electronic portfolio should allow for documenting the varying means in which programs articulate, deliver, and gather evidence of the student learning.

After program leaders have articulated program outcomes, identified the method in which they will deliver the outcomes, and specified the way the outcomes will be evaluated, they design the electronic student portfolio template with this information. To continue with our example, we will use the leadership program outcome of "Students will be able to debate accurately and clearly varying points of views of a selected topic." The way in which this skill is taught is through workshops. The evidence of this learning is gathered in student government debates and in presentations made to the faculty senate. These naturally occurring platforms are loaded into the electronic portfolio template as assignments to the student.

In other words, in order for the co-curricular professional to know that the learning has occurred, the student must enter the artifacts of the debates into the portfolio under the appropriate outcome for the co-curricular specialist to evaluate later. The program leader instructs the student to load these artifacts in after the student has been taught the content that should be evident in the artifact. The student loads the presentations prepared for the debate and possibly video clips of the actual debate itself into the portfolio. The student may also have provided the program leader with a self-evaluation of how well he or she thinks he or she did in "clearly and accurately" debating the selected topic.

The same can hold true for the political science professor. The professor sets up a template for the outcome of "Students will be able to apply their viewpoints effectively, efficiently, and persuasively in both writing and speaking to issues of public policy." The professor's naturally occurring artifacts are classroom presentations, essays from assignments, and classroom debates. The student is instructed to upload their artifacts in accordance with the assignment timeline and the instructor evaluates them for the extent to which they meet the learning outcome.

If both the political scientist and co-curricular specialist have these example learning outcomes tied to their institutional learning principles of "speaking," the programs are now also gathering evidence of how their programs are contributing to meeting that institutional goal. In addition, they are gathering evidence in a manner that will help them know what to improve in their programs should the learning not meet their expectations.

Furthermore, imagine a student who is both in the university leadership co-curricular program and a political science major. That student may alert the political science professor and the student leadership instructor to the fact that both programs have shared outcomes around speaking. The student may invite both to evaluate the learning artifacts from each other's assignments. Now the instructors in both programs are aware of the learning that is complemented and enhanced by each other's program; thus, the program leaders may choose to collaborate on future assignments or to collaborate on the criteria they are using to evaluate each assignment.

The electronic student portfolio facilitated this example of connecting student learning in the curricular and co-curricular programs. The end result for these programs and for the students involved in both of them can be enhanced awareness of how each is contributing to institutional core learning values as well as the student understanding the connection and transference of learning from the co-curricular to the curricular program and vice versa.

Criteria for Evaluation

An additional area for collaboration of student learning outcomes among curricular and co-curricular programs and across the co-curricular program is the sharing of criteria for evaluating a particular outcome. Criteria are a "set of indicators, markers, guides, or a list of measures or qualities that will help you know when a student has met an outcome" (Bresciani, Zelna, and Anderson, 2004, p. 29). When the criteria are created to measure the student learning in a particular program for a specific outcome, such as ethical reasoning in student leadership, the criteria used by one program may not be shared by another program, even though it has an outcome related to ethical reasoning.

One way to share the criteria for evaluation of an artifact of learning requested from a student in a program is to post the criteria for evaluation in the template of the student portfolio. As another colleague at your invitation, for example in Residence Life, sees the artifact of learning for an outcome that shares a value with his or her program (such as ethical reasoning), the colleague can see how you evaluate the artifact from your criteria. Over time, your colleague may come to share the criteria you have developed or help you refine the criteria so that it works for both of your programs. The purpose of all this is for the student, over time, to better understand what it means to reason ethically in the co-curricular environment. This also allows the co-curricular specialists to evaluate how students are improving their ethical reasoning skills, whether they attended one workshop in student activities and two in residence life, or three in the student leadership program.

Criteria for Selecting a Student Electronic Portfolio

There are many student electronic portfolios on the market. This chapter has presented a detailed illustration of one of the products available. Prior to selecting any electronic portfolios for the Huba and Freed model however, it is important to get answers to the following questions:

- Does the electronic portfolio allow for the documentation of individual student learning?
- Does the electronic portfolio allow for the documented student learning to be linked to program outcomes?
- Does the electronic portfolio allow for the documented student learning to be linked to institutional learning principles?
- Can the evidence of student learning be shared across discipline and division program outcomes? In other words, can one program's student

learning evidence be linked to another program that may have a shared outcome?

- Can the criteria for the evaluation of student learning be documented within the electronic portfolio and linked to the outcome that it is evaluating?
- What kind of feedback options on student work are provided to the evaluator?
- Can the student respond to the evaluator's feedback?
- Can an external evaluator or an evaluator from another program comment on the learning artifact?
- Can the student evaluate his or her own learning artifact?
- How easy is the electronic portfolio to use for the student? For the faculty member? For the co-curricular specialist?
- Can artifacts from course-management software be uploaded into the electronic student portfolio?
- Can the electronic student portfolio be linked to assessment-management software?
- What kinds of reports can be generated from the electronic portfolio? Do those reports assist the program with its evaluation?
- Can the reports be made ready to post right onto a program's Web site?
- How easily can the electronic student portfolio reports be imported into other kinds of reporting templates, such as annual reports?
- What kind of training will be required? What kind does the vendor provide?
- What kind of server is required? How much space is needed?
- What kind of browser is required?
- What are the security protections?
- What kind of ongoing support is required? What does the vendor provide?

References

ACPA. *Student Learning Imperative: Implications for Student Affairs.* 1996. http://www.acpa.nche.edu/sli/sli.htm. Accessed June 17, 2004.

Alverno College. "The Diagnostic Digital Portfolio." 2001. http://www.alverno.edu/academics/ddp.html. Accessed June 17, 2004.

Association of American Colleges and Universities (AAC&U). "Greater Expectations: A New Vision for Learning as a Nation Goes to College." 2003. http://www.aacu-edu.org/gex/index.cfm. Accessed June 17, 2004.

Bresciani, M. J. "Outcomes Assessment in Student Affairs: Moving Beyond Satisfaction to Student Learning and Development." National Association for Student Personnel Administrators, *NetResults,* December 2002. http://www.naspa.org/netresults/index.cfm. Accessed June 17, 2004.

Bresciani, M. J. "Identifying Projects that Deliver Outcomes and Provide a Means of Assessment: A Concept Mapping Checklist." National Association for Student Personnel Administrators, *NetResults,* December 2003. http://www.naspa.org/membership/mem/nr/article.cfm?id=1291. Accessed June 17, 2004.

Bresciani, M. J., Zelna, C. L., and Anderson, J. A. *Assessing Student Learning and Development: A Handbook for Practitioners.* Washington, D.C.: NASPA, 2004.

Ewell, P. T. "Specific Roles of Assessment Within this Larger Vision." Paper presented at the Assessment Institute at IUPUI (Indiana University-Purdue University-Indianapolis), 2003.

Huba, M. E., and Freed, J. E. *Learner-Centered Assessment on College Campuses: Shifting the Focus from Teaching to Learning.* Boston: Allyn and Bacon, 2000.

Kruger, K. "Electronic Portfolios: The Next Big Thing?" *The Leadership Exchange, 2.* Washington D.C.: NASPA, Spring 2003.

Palomba, C. A., and Banta, T. W. *Assessment Essentials: Planning, Implementing, and Improving Assessment in Higher Education.* San Francisco: Jossey-Bass, 1999.

MARILEE J. BRESCIANI is assistant vice president for institutional assessment at Texas A & M University.

Changing technologies give students new ways to stay connected, be entertained, and interact with their institution. Student affairs practitioners must find ways to use these emerging technologies to further their educational goals and purposes.

The Way Technology Changes How We Do What We Do

Maria Tess Shier

Changing technologies have affected nearly every aspect of society today, and higher education is no exception. From e-mailed e-postcards and college look books to online applications for admission and from online orientation programs to e-learning courses led by a professor located across the country, students today have a high comfort level with technology as a part of their everyday life and have come to expect certain services to be automated, online, and available twenty-four hours a day.

Processes once paper based have been streamlined and timelines shortened by the use of technology in such areas as registration and application. But just as certain areas are improved by technological advances, a range of other issues or problems arise as a result of changing technology. File sharing, Internet addiction, and technology's effects on campus community are three critical issues for student affairs practitioners to be aware of and responsive to.

File Sharing

In fall 2004, the Recording Industry Association of America (RIAA) filed a $98 billion lawsuit against four college students (Shaw and Shaw, 2003), serving as an effort both for legal retribution against those already thought to be engaged in illegal file sharing and as a message to others who might consider it in the future. With 6.4 million users of file-sharing services in the United States alone, the RIAA and other owners of copyrighted material have a vested interest in protecting their business assets (Kessler, 2005).

Student use of file sharing has been a topic of interest to both businesses and scholars, and in November 2004, a study of 265 Michigan State University students was conducted to identify reasons that students engaged in file-sharing activities.

The results of the survey indicated that, contrary to RIAA public statements, there was a "relatively minor role played by economic factors" in terms of student motivations to engage in illegal file sharing (Carlson, 2004, p. A32). The primary reasons students cited for engaging in file sharing were the related social interactions associated with the act of file sharing, such as chatting online about a musical genre or chatting with others who share a common musical interest, particularly conversations related to finding out about new music (Carlson, 2004). Some programs allow for user-to-user e-mail communication, furthering the social connection from the relatively anonymous chat rooms to a more personal, one-to-one communication, building a cyber-community for users.

Although officials at RIAA maintain that economic factors were of primary influence in a student's decision to download music illegally, the Michigan State University study indicates that institutions may want to look at ways to support music and file sharing within their legal abilities, not only as a way to prevent future legal action, but also as a way of fostering community and connections on campus (Shaw and Shaw, 2003). The study also showed that, for students with thousands of songs downloaded, the threats of losing Internet access or expulsion were stronger deterrents than the threat of lawsuits (Carlson, 2004).

Another, nationwide, study of six hundred participants found that, while most young adults (55 percent) believed that file sharing of copyrighted material was in fact illegal, 54 percent simultaneously believed that it should not be restricted (Carlson, 2004). This study was one in a series of quarterly surveys conducted by the New Jersey Institute of Technology. Seventeen percent of respondents who identified as between eighteen and thirty-four years of age had engaged in illegal file sharing; the closest next usage was 5 percent of thirty-five to fifty-four-year-olds having engaged in similar activities. The disconnect between identifying file sharing as illegal yet still wanting it to be unregulated and widely available fits with student development theory, such as the work of Perry on students' intellectual development (1968), or Kohlberg's moral development model (1969), and speaks to the challenges of changing student behaviors. These theories identify different stages of development where students may feel that rules are contextual and relative and begin to rely less on authorities when deciding right from wrong. Therefore, as institutions look at ways to legally support student interest in file sharing by fostering an online music or other type of file-sharing community, they also may want to consider strong policies against misuse of the system as an effective deterrent to excessive or illegal behavior and to look at file sharing as a real-world case study for ethical development. A subscription service for file sharing is one type of service currently available to institutions at a cost, similar to a library subscription to a journal or periodical, and is used at more than twenty-five institutions to date. In at attempt to support a highly connected community within legal parameters, some institutions are creating student behavioral policies or departments to manage this effort, to be discussed later.

Responding to Student Violations. Although the Digital Millennium Copyright Act (DMCA) states that universities are not required to monitor the activity that occurs on their online servers, it does require colleges and universities to comply with "the notice and take down" provisions of the DMCA once aware of illegal activities (Shaw and Shaw, 2003, p. 24). The 2005 Su-preme Court's unanimous ruling that file-sharing sites such as Grokster or Morpheus can be held liable for their user's piracy further hints at the need for institutions to acknowledge their responsibility in monitoring the technology and access they provide to their students, faculty, and staff (*Metro-Goldwyn-Mayer Studios Inc., et al. v. Grokster, LTD, et al.*, 2005).

The combined ease of file sharing and the wide bandwidth technology of college and university Internet systems contribute to the proliferation of peer-to-peer file sharing. As mentioned earlier, there are a number of other motivational factors as to why college-age students engage in file sharing at a rate significantly higher than other segments of the population (Carlson, 2004). How to respond to this behavior has even more varied responses. Tracy B. Mitrano, director of Cornell University's Computer Policy and Law Program, has proposed the following steps for an institution to begin addressing the problem of illegal file-sharing (Mitrano, 2004, p. B16):

Develop a statement of intent to comply with the Digital Millennium Copyright Act of 1998.

Determine if the institution wishes to monitor and respond to any copyright infringement they find occurring on their service or merely see themselves as the service provider and therefore not liable for the actions of the user-students.

Create protocol for responding to copyright infringement for students (on campus and off campus) and for employees—groups that must be addressed differently due to the institution's relationship with the individuals.

Develop a policy as to how the institution would respond to a subpoena seeking identification information on specific individuals suspected of engaging in illegal file sharing.

Protocols might include temporarily restricting Internet access, issuing cease-and-desist orders, or other judicial sanctions. It is noted that when an institution identifies (or has identified for it by an external agency such as RIAA) students suspected of infringing on copyrighted material and deals with them through the campus judicial system, there are no reported repeat offenders (Shaw and Shaw, 2003). The campus judicial system seems to educate the student successfully to the point of a change in behavior. In some cases, a well-worded call or e-mail message from an Internet ethics officer to someone merely suspected of Internet misuse can result in the student self-regulating his or her behavior and voluntarily ceasing illegal activity.

Because file sharing can be used to support the educational mission of the institution, it should not immediately be discounted as something to be simply shut down. For example, at Berklee College of Music, a program called Berklee Shares provides lessons in music performance, business, production, and other related areas. The program provides the lessons through a file-sharing program for cost, and the content of the lessons are provided in a protected format that the purchaser cannot alter (Foster, 2003). As such, Berklee Shares has been able to meet its institutional mission of music education through new technologies. Other institutions use file sharing to promote student interactions by sharing classroom notes or viewing artwork or other printed material no longer in printed circulation. Institutions must find a way to support these legitimate uses of file sharing as they look to limit the illegitimate uses available to students.

Technology and Ethics. Advancements in online research methods have greatly increased our ability to seek out information independently through powerful online search engines. For students, this has meant a desire to complete 100 percent of the research needed for their senior thesis online from the comfort of their room, never stepping foot into the library itself. It has also meant that students have a variety of options for unethical behavior related to research. Unlike the technology of file sharing, which can have legitimate academic benefits and therefore is still under debate as to its use on campuses, cybercheating is unarguably a contradiction to the mission and purpose of any college or university.

Students today have the ability to purchase and download a research paper in minutes; to cut and paste directly from an online resource into their own term paper, rather than paraphrasing and citing the author; and to copy an unprotected PowerPoint or Web document by simply changing a few identifiers of ownership. As fast as TurnItIn.com can generate a new tool to help professors identify purchased papers, the papers4you.com site can generate a new URL and a new paper to sell.

The 2003 National Survey of Student Engagement reported that 87 percent of students who completed the survey reported copying information directly from the Internet without properly citing the source "at least some of the time" (Sterngold, 2004, p. 18). As universities expand the availability of their online libraries and as Google develops partnerships with institutions to increase the searchability of a school's online library, it can be reasonably expected that cybercheating and digital plagiarism will increase, either in the frequency of cheating or in the scope of cheating methods used. As such, colleges and universities need to find ways to educate students on proper expectations of academic honesty related to cybercheating. The anonymity of online resources means college and universities must teach today's students new expectations and methods of proper online research and its responsible and ethical use. Disturbed by file-sharing issues and other inappropriate use of the campus servers, some colleges and universities have created offices to provide guidance for online usage.

Offices have been established at the University of Maryland at College Park, Northeastern University, and the State University of New York at Buffalo, among others, to address the wide variety of student behavioral issues related to the Internet. In addition to dealing with the ever-present file-sharing issues, such offices are equipped to deal with activities as diverse as offering preventive educational programs on proper online research to finding a student who has hacked into a secure server. They will use existing campus judicial methods to address the actions of a student sending harassing e-mails as they simultaneously assist the recipient of the harassing e-mails by setting up a blocking function and making referrals as needed, such as to the counseling center.

Smaller institutions, however, may not have the ability to create an entire office for Internet ethics, and the responsibility for addressing inappropriate actions disproportionably falls to student affairs departments, such as residence life or the judicial office. Therefore, administrators in all student affairs functional areas should have a working awareness of campus policies about Internet misuse and proper procedures to follow when working with students in this area.

Administrators seeking to address digital dishonesty can find help in the following articles:

- "Designing Online Courses to Discourage Dishonesty" (Christe, 2003)
- "Confronting Plagiarism" (Sterngold, 2004)
- "Next-Generation: Educational Technology versus the Lecture" (Foreman, 2003) and related articles in that issue of EDUCAUSE Review

Internet Addiction

Some roommates who cannot speak civilly to one another sit back-to-back as they argue over AOL IM. Other students arrive to their 8 A.M. English class blurry eyed after having stayed up all night playing linked Internet games, such as Halo, online against four other students, each in a different state. And there are the students who are so engrossed in their time online that they miss the hours of the dining hall, happy hour with friends, and perhaps even seeing direct sunlight for several consecutive days.

What classifies a student as simply highly wired versus engaging in unhealthy and possibility addictive Internet-related activities? There are no clear answers or guidelines. As with avid television watchers or those who regularly get lost in a good book, the difference between simply intense and in-depth enjoyment of a hobby and involvement that has negative consequences is narrow. Do students who watch four or more hours of television a day suffer from TV addiction, or are they are budding TV producers in the works? Is excessive TV watching really just a manifestation of something else, say boredom or depression?

It is difficult to identify consistent data on what is classified as excessive Internet use, Internet abuse, or even Internet addiction disorder (*Chronicle of Higher Education,* 2003; Grohol, 2005; Holmes, 2005; Mental Help Net, 2005). Internet addiction disorder (IAD) can be defined by the individual's compulsive dependency on a particular kind of Internet-based stimulation to the degree that obtaining that stimulation becomes the central, and perhaps the only, focus of their life (Mental Help Net, 2005).

Whether or not IAD is a true disorder (similar to substance addiction, for example) is debatable and is often defined by the results of the Internet usage rather than just the student's actions. If academic achievement drops or if students significantly change their patterns of social or recreational interactions, they could be in need of professional or academic assistance, but not necessarily addicted. Others who spend significant time on the Internet gambling may actually have a gambling addiction that has manifested itself through online outlets. The question becomes whether the student is addicted to the Internet itself or to the stimulation of the online activity in which the student is engaged.

Although student affairs professionals may not be able to identify a student officially or formally as having IAD, it is still critical to know what the warning signs may be. It is important to note that college students spend significantly more time online than other age categories in the United States (Grohol, 2005). This may be a function of generational differences, high-speed (and often free) Internet access on campus, and the amount of academic coursework requiring students to go online, but it does point to the need to assess each student individually.

For campuses, this means staff need to be prepared to identify when a student may have IAD or a less severe level of Internet use or abuse. Staff also need to be prepared to decipher if the addiction is to the Internet itself as opposed to a subset of what is provided through the Internet and then make the appropriate referral for the student. For staff who live in residence halls or otherwise have daily student contact, it may be easier to identify the changes in students' physical appearances that indicate other changes in behavior. Resident assistants may be best placed to identify students with Internet usage concerns, so incorporating training about IAD into RA training should be considered, just as RAs and staff receive training about other compulsive habits and disorders.

Because much of what students do online is akin to socializing, it can be hard for students to see their online behaviors as negative. Chatting online does not seem too different from teens talking for hours on the phone in the 1980s. Watching a live concert broadcast isn't too far removed from being at the actual concert in person. "Googling" someone is just a quick, anonymous version of asking friends if they know anything about that cute redhead in English 101. So it is important to understand that what professionals may see as intense behavior with negative consequences, students may see as the modern ways of communicating, interacting, dating, and learning. Student affairs professionals should be aware of these new online communities if they wish to remain current about the factors affecting their students' lives.

Building Community Through Technology

They connect nightly with friends far away on IM, sometimes one-to-one and sometimes in a chat room. They connect with their local friend by posting an away message saying which bar they'll be at tonight and to "cell me." They text each other from across the bar, as it's too crowded to meet halfway, and even if they could, it'd be too loud to really talk in person. And they then share photos of that night's escapades by posting their digital photo album online through a link on their public profile (user name and password openly provided, of course).

Technology is a way of life for students today. Beyond registering for classes and researching papers online, students' ability to stay connected with old friends and find new ones through online methods means colleges and universities need to rethink the way they attempt to build community for their students. No longer will ice cream socials in the residence hall lobby be sufficient to bring students together, despite the everlasting lure of free food for college students. Rather, should colleges and universities try to find ways to use student-friendly technology to be a part of the community-building process?

Facebook.com. Facebook.com is one example of how students have sought out ways to create community outside the institution. Similar to the Freshman Look Book idea popular a few decades ago, Facebook.com. was created by a group of students at Harvard College in February 2004 as a college dating service, but the online program now has nearly six hundred colleges participating and more than 2.4 million users, according to their Web site (Rosen, 2005).

Facebook.com allows students to post a profile with pictures and personal information, such as hobbies and interests. It also allows them to invite others to be listed as "friends" who are counted on their sites and can post messages about them on their "wall"—literally a place where people can come and openly write any comments about the student. (Students do have the ability to edit out any comments they would not like to have up on their wall.) Social nets allow students to connect and link with other students based on similar interests, such as a favorite band or sports team.

As the students' definition of community moves beyond geographic and physical limitations, Facebook.com provides one way for students to find others with common interests, feel as though they are part of a larger community, and also find out about others in their classes. Browsing online photos of others with a similar class schedule is much less intimidating than asking friends if they know the name of your crush and, after reading the profile, students may find their own way to spark up a conversation or find their interest has waned. Because of this power to connect with others, the appeal of Facebook.com has moved beyond just students to faculty and staff.

For professors and administrators, Facebook.com can be a way of connecting with students—especially important at institutions where student-teacher contact can be limited. Some professors have been providing their students with their IM screen name for students to ask questions online rather than coming to office hours in person. Professors or administrators who post a profile on Facebook.com find that it can be a good way for students to get to know them beyond the academic setting, seeing what hobbies or interests the student may share with the professor, which may encourage the feeling of a professor being approachable. University of Iowa President, David J. Skorton, posted a profile and received thousands of requests to be listed as a "friend" on students' profiles (Liu, 2005). About thirty Yale professors have profiles, as well as more than one hundred faculty and staff at Duke University (Duboff, 2005; Liu, 2005). Although not yet having an academic purpose, Facebook.com provides a way for students to create online communities and networks with peers as well as faculty and staff.

Problems have arisen from Facebook.com profiles, including stalking and groups that may focus on activities the institution does not want to encourage, such as locating parties for underage students or groups that degrade specific minority groups (Dutton, 2005). Although the institution cannot regulate what their students post on Facebook.com, they may have to deal with the repercussions of the site, such as by addressing feelings of being racially targeted or being stalked by another student after having posted one's real phone number or e-mail address. Because students do not know who might look at their profile, the site offers a variety of privacy options to the user.

RateMyProfessor.com. Although many schools may already use the traditional scantron-pencil-in-the-bubbles end-of-term teacher evaluation, the use and effectiveness of the results vary widely from institution to institution. As such, students have found their own way to share opinions about professors—through RateMyProfessor.com. Ratings, indicated by smiley faces, are calculated on a five-point scale in five categories, such as "easiness" and "clarity." The site also allows students to indicate if teachers are "hot" by the use of a chili pepper icon.

Although the ability to rate the professor is not restricted to students who actually have taken a class with the professor, the site remains popular with students. Although students are the primary target audience for the site, professors and administrators have been known to check their ratings. An administrator at the University of Waterloo (Canada) went so far as to informally compare the ratings of that school's teachers found on

RateMyProfessor.com to the results of their internal teacher evalua-tions. His findings indicated a general correlation between the scores on RateMyProfessor.com and their course evaluations: of the sixteen Distinguished Teacher Award winners in 2003, fifteen were also highly rated on RateMyProfessor.com (Essajee, 2002).

Other Technology Influences. Student government elections have been changed in recent years by technology. At the Ohio State University (OSU), the switch from paper voting to online voting in 2001 increased voter turnout from 6 percent to 13 percent. OSU's graduate school elections saw a similar increase, from 1 percent voter turnout to 7 percent (Read, 2005). But the influence of technology on elections starts well before voting day, as candidates use the Internet as a powerful campaign tool.

Campaign Web sites are used to give candidate profiles, indicate platform issues, promote debate events, and take quick polls of student concerns. Students at George Mason University went beyond campaign Web sites in the 2005 spring elections. Campaign groups used both Facebook.com social nets and IM to promote themselves. Facebook social nets indicated supporters, and one campaign Web site provided a link to download an IM icon of the presidential and vice presidential candidates' photos to one's own profile. Campus-based blogs were also used to discuss platform issues, the content of candidate-sponsored blogs reiterating blog content during candidate debates, both to prove support for a position and to attack an opponent's position (Read, 2005). At the University of Minnesota, blogs affected the 2005 spring elections by providing both a political platform for candidates and an outlet for critics to spread their views widely and without external editing. Even blogs of those unaffiliated with any candidate gained readership once the author began commenting on the upcoming elections (Haugen, 2005). All this new technology, however, did not stop Homer Simpson, Jose Cuervo, and Mickey Mouse from getting a few write-in votes.

Conclusion

Technology changes the way students live, learn, and interact with their colleges and universities. Accordingly, institutions must change the way they use technology, both in how they provide day-to-day services for students and how they connect with students in less structured, but equally meaningful, ways. Technological advances may have decreased human contact in some parts of university life, but savvy faculty and staff are finding ways to use technology in other ways to increase student-staff and student-faculty contact and to create communities in new ways. Providing legal alternatives to illegal file sharing has a cost-benefit calculation the institution can quantify, especially in light of increased legal action by RIAA and others. Institutions must find ways to address this ongoing problem within their existing technological—and judicial—structures.

Unlike the purchase of a music download service, using free services such as Facebook.com, AOL IM, or RateMyProfessor.com involves little financial investment for institutions but can greatly increase the connections to students on campus. These modern methods of community building are the ways students today are meeting, communicating, and building community. Just as how knowing the latest hit song or fashion trend can provide a way to connect with a student, these online methods provide multiple ways of knowing and connecting with students. Staff should have a working awareness of Internet addiction and related behaviors, especially when interacting with students in an online environment, but will likely find that being a highly connected professional is of great value to their work and their relationships with students.

References

Carlson, S. "Why They Pirate: Study Says Students Aren't in It for the Free Songs." *Chronicle of Higher Education*, May 21, 2004, p. A32.

Christe, B. "Designing Online Courses to Discourage Dishonesty." *Educause Quarterly*, 2003, 26(4), 540–558.

Chronicle of Higher Education. "Internet 'Addiction' Is Symptom, Not Cause, of Problems in Life, Study Finds." *Chronicle of Higher Education*, July 18, 2003, p. A29.

Duboff, J. "'Poke' Your Prof: Faculty Discovers thefacebook.com." *Yale Daily News*, March 24, 2005, pp. 1, 4.

Dutton, C. "U. Kansas Facebook User Reports Stalking." *University Daily Kansan*, Feb. 10, 2005. http://www.kansan.com/stories/2005/feb/10/news_campus_facebook. Accessed Sept. 14, 2005.

Essajee, S. "The Person at the Front of the Class Comes in Four Varieties." *Imprint*, June 14, 2002.

Foreman, J. "Next-Generation: Educational Technology Versus the Lecture." *EDUCAUSE* Review, July/August 2003, pp. 12–22.

Foster, A. "Boston Music College Offers Free Lessons Through File Sharing on the Internet." *Chronicle of Higher Education*, December 5, 2003, p. A24.

Grohol, J. M. "Internet Addiction Guide." *Dr. Grohol's Psych Central*. April 16, 2005. http://psychcentral.com/netaddiction/. Accessed June 1, 2005.

Haugen, B. "Bloggers and thefacebook.com Are Taking Part in MSA Elections." *The Minnesota Daily*, March 28, 2005. http://www.mndaily.com/articles/2005/03/28/63831. Accessed Sept. 14, 2005.

Holmes, L. "What Is 'Normal' Internet Use?" *About, Inc.* http://mentalhealth.about.com/cs/sexaddict/a/normalinet_p.htm. Accessed May 13, 2005.

Kessler, M. "Court Limits File Sharing, Display of Commandments." *USA Today*, June 28, 2005, p. 1.

Kohlberg, L. "Stage and Sequence: The Cognitive-Development Approach to Socialization." In D. A. Goslin (ed.), *Handbook of Socialization Theory and Research*. Chicago: Rand McNally, 1969.

Liu, M. "Duke Professors Join Facebook Craze." *The Chronicle*, Feb. 25, 2005. http://www.chronicle.duke.edu/vnews/display.v/ART/2005/02/25/421f32add5086. Accessed Sept. 14, 2005.

Mental Help Net. "Internet Addiction." http://www.mentalhelpnet.com/poc/center_index.php?id=66. Accessed June 1, 2005.

Metro-Goldwyn-Mayer Studios Inc., et al. v. Grokster, LTD, et al., 380 F.3d 1154 (2005).

Mitrano, T. "How Colleges Should Respond to File-Sharing Charges." *Chronicle of Higher Education,* June 24, 2004, p. B16.

Perry, W. G., Jr. *Forms of Intellectual and Ethical Development in the College Years: A Scheme.* New York: Holt, Rinehart and Winston, 1968.

Read, B. "Vote Early, Vote Online." *Chronicle of Higher Education,* May 13, 2005, p. A27.

Rosen, E. "Student's Start-Up Draws Attention and $13 Million." *New York Times,* May 26, 2005. http://www.nytimes.com/2005/05/26/business/26sbiz.html?ex=1126843200&en=a3f4dad9ff6bb603&ei=5070&ex=1117771200&en=377ee030cd546112&ei=5040&partner=MOREOVERNEWS. Accessed Sept. 14, 2005.

Shaw, M. H., and Shaw, B. "Copyright in the Age of Photocopiers, Word Processors, and the Internet." *Change,* Nov./Dec. 2003, pp. 21–33.

Sterngold, A. "Confronting Plagiarism." *Change,* May/June, 2004, pp. 16–27.

MARIA TESS SHIER is director of the James. E. Scott Academy for Leadership and Executive Effectiveness at the National Association of Student Personnel Administrators (NASPA).

8

The author reviews the evolution of Web services—from information sharing to transactional to relationship building—and the progression from first-generation to fourth-generation Web sites.

Weaving Silos—A Leadership Challenge: A Cross-Functional Team Approach to Supporting Web-Based Student Services

Gary L. Kleemann

Back in the dark ages—say, before 1995—students didn't have easy access to e-mail, cell phones that took pictures, or instant messaging; nor did they have ready and easy access to something called the World Wide Web. Student services, whether those delivered by academic affairs units (such as library services or tutoring), business affairs units (such as fee payment or parking renewal), or student affairs units (such as registration, career services, personal counseling, or voting in student elections) were all delivered to the student customer by having the student physically come to the place of the service to receive it. This often meant long lines or services that required advance appointments and planning on the part of the student receiving the service. Desktop computers were just beginning to be part of the experience for student affairs professionals. Beginning in the 1990s this paradigm began to change.

During the 1990s, desktop computers went from being very special items for only a few to becoming ubiquitous. The first truly usable version of Windows—version 3.0—was shipped in May 1990 (Freidman, 2005). The computer screen changed from a somewhat cryptic, character-based screen to a graphical user interface. In the mid-1990s people were introduced to the World Wide Web, and everyone learned about something called a Web browser. Netscape, the first broadly popular commercial browser to surf the Internet, went public in August 1995 and changed the landscape forever (Freidman, 2005). Some students and faculty began to develop their own Web pages. A few brave offices hired students to help them develop Web pages for their offices and even a smaller number learned how to write HTML code. Somehow a computer guru developed in almost every office—someone who liked computers and took responsibility for helping everyone else learn how to use these new tools. E-mail went from being a novelty to something that everyone depends on today. Many different services were automated and computerized. A comprehensive strategy for using and supporting these new tools was unheard of at the beginning of the decade but was considered a necessity on most campuses by the end of the decade. Thus, a dramatic paradigm shift occurred during the decade of the 1990s.

In 2000, outlining his vision for the future of computing technology, Microsoft chairman Bill Gates said that the terminal-mainframe, character-based PC era, the graphical user-interface era, and the browsing era would be followed by an era marked by highly personalized Web sites compiling data from multiple sources. In 2000, the computing device is central. Each device contains different data, which are specifically configured for that device. In the future, users become central, having secure access to their information anywhere and on any device (Gottesman, 2000). Now, several years later, Gates's vision has come true—at least from the technology point of view. We have hardware and software that will allow users to become central, but we have not yet quite figured out how to manage the human side of it.

J. James Wager, assistant vice provost for enrollment management and university registrar at Pennsylvania State University, recently noted, "While information technology has had a significant impact on the Net Generation, practices and expectations within the academy remain relatively unchanged. Classes continue to be taught by instructors in classrooms. Students are expected to navigate complex administrative processes. In many ways, the academy continues to be staff-centric. Although some colleges and universities have demonstrated measurable progress in moving toward a student-centered philosophy, many have not. Their administrative structure, information systems, and approach to the delivery of student services continue to represent the traditional hierarchy experienced by previous generations of students" (Wager, 2005, pp. 10.1–10.2)

Technology and the Web have progressed through several stages over the past decade, so that we are now able to become more student-centric in our organizations. Our organizations need to become more student-centric if we are to meet the challenges of the future, but for far too many of us, student affairs is still using a traditional organizational hierarchy. This must change. Student affairs leaders are needed to take us to a new student-centric future in our organizations. Let's take a look at the short history of how Web technology has evolved and what that evolution might mean to student affairs and our organizations.

Stages of Web Site Development

Institutions typically have gone through several styles, stages, or generations as they have worked to develop Web-based student services. Different observers have seen this in different ways, but all seem to agree that there is a developmental process in play.

In an online article, Janet Jackson, co-owner of a Web design company, has suggested that there are three styles of Web sites (listed in order of complexity):

Informational. These sites are online marketing brochures or branding tools that invite visitors to learn about the organization and its offerings. This is how most Web sites start out and what most people think of as the purpose of their departmental Web site.

Transactional. These are e-commerce sites. They can range from selling one product (textbooks, for example) to offering a service (online registration and fee payment) to providing services that support brick-and-mortar, face-to-face services to establishing fully functioning online services. Transactional sites are geared for visitors ready to conduct business. This is how colleagues in business affairs may think of campus Web sites.

Relationship Builders. These sites work to develop relationships with visitors over time. They encourage involvement and two-way communications, providing valuable data or expertise while requesting and capturing visitor information in return. Such sites offer interactivity, provide educational or time-sensitive information, and motivate repeat visits. That means that people must invest in updating the content. These sites are designed for organizations or organizational units that benefit or grow by interacting with those they serve (Krotz, 2005).

Generations

Darlene Burnett (2002) has identified four generations of Web-site development—each with its own view or perspective. They are the institutional view, the customer view, the Web portal, and high-touch and high-tech stage.

First Generation—The Institutional View or Brochure Stage. In this stage, the Web was used as an electronic brochure, where static printed material was transformed into static electronic material. Tons of information about the campus was placed, brochure-like, on the Web for all to see—one-way publishing. Staff and student directories and eventually some critical information, such as catalogs and event information, maps, and directions to campus, were placed there. Anything that could be published on paper was also given a home on the Web.

Material usually was organized much like the organizational structure of the college or university, with each organizational unit placing information about itself on the site. There most often was little or no coordination between units, with each unit developing its own look and feel. Material was organized and presented from the institution's point of view. As a result, navigation of the Web site was often confusing. Keeping information current and accurate was an ongoing and difficult challenge.

Second Generation—The Customer View or Transaction Stage. In this stage, the Web site becomes more interactive and allows for customers (students, faculty, parents, alumni, and others) to actually transact some business. People can fill out and submit forms online, order services, pay bills, and transact other business.

Information is still organized by institutional unit and presented from the institution's point of view. The Web site remains institution-centric. There is limited interaction between the Web site and various institutional databases. The site is not personalized to the end user.

Third Generation—The Web Portal or Personalized and Interactive Stage. In this stage, a Web portal interacts with the various institutional databases to build the Web site on the fly specifically for each student. Every student experiences it a little differently. The site is personalized, customized, and interactive, providing services and information that the student customer needs or wants. The page is populated with information specifically about that individual student (major, year in school, resident or commuter, co-curricular interests, and so on). The student can personalize the site even more to meet his or her needs and interests. Web site navigation is organized to meet the needs of each particular student customer. This provides the beginnings of establishing a one-to-one relationship between the student and the institution. It is student-centric and not institution-centric. Routine services are available 24/7, and person-to-person services are usually easily available at times convenient for the student customer.

Fourth Generation—The High-Tech and High-Touch Stage. In this stage the focus is on creating a positive experience and developing a relationship between the student and the institution. These Web sites are highly customized (from information in campus databases) and personalized (by the end user). They use data compiled from multiple sources and they provide quality services 24 hours a day, 7 days a week. They may provide text interaction, with personalized, proactive communications and recommendations. They seek to develop relationships with the end user and enhance community. They may well involve the use of e-portfolios. They may provide step-by-step help with advising. They may let the end user know, for example, about things like registration dates, fee deadlines, and campus lectures on topics relevant to the student in a timely manner. They work to enhance a sense of community. They provide real-time interaction with the institution and a high level of "high touch" (Burnett, 2002).

Ellen-Earle Chaffee, President of Valley City State University (North Dakota), has noted that "The greatest benefit of technologies is not bridging distance but supporting mass customization of learning with convenience, responsiveness, and quality" (Chaffee, 2005, p. 7). It is all about the experience.

Figure 8.1. Traditional Organization Chart

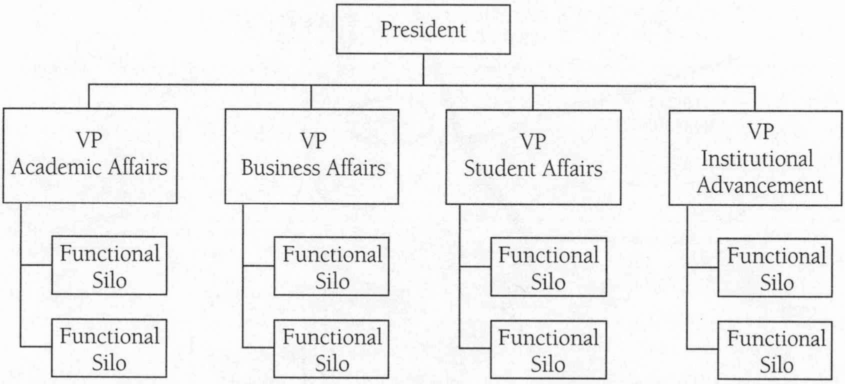

```
                        ┌───────────┐
                        │ President │
                        └───────────┘

┌─────────────┐  ┌─────────────┐  ┌─────────────┐  ┌─────────────┐
│     VP      │  │     VP      │  │     VP      │  │     VP      │
│ Academic    │  │ Business    │  │ Student     │  │Institutional│
│ Affairs     │  │ Affairs     │  │ Affairs     │  │ Advancement │
└─────────────┘  └─────────────┘  └─────────────┘  └─────────────┘

 ┌──────────┐    ┌──────────┐    ┌──────────┐    ┌──────────┐
 │Functional│    │Functional│    │Functional│    │Functional│
 │  Silo    │    │  Silo    │    │  Silo    │    │  Silo    │
 └──────────┘    └──────────┘    └──────────┘    └──────────┘

 ┌──────────┐    ┌──────────┐    ┌──────────┐    ┌──────────┐
 │Functional│    │Functional│    │Functional│    │Functional│
 │  Silo    │    │  Silo    │    │  Silo    │    │  Silo    │
 └──────────┘    └──────────┘    └──────────┘    └──────────┘
```

Paradigm Shifts, Vision, and Leadership

"Organizations are not built to serve customers but to preserve internal order. The internal structure means very little to the customer—and may serve as a barrier. Organizational charts are vertical and serving the customer is horizontal" (Burnett, 2002, pp. 3–4).

We often see our organization as a neatly organized, well-oiled machine. In the traditional culture of higher education, services are delivered in person and each office is focused on a single area of responsibility (functional silos). Figure 8.1 shows the way many of our organizations are structured.

While it may well not be the case on your campus, in far too many places, separate, uncoordinated departments work to do their best to serve students. Overly specialized staff are not able to provide holistic service. The result is that students can be bounced from office to office.

All too often there are limited communication and coordination between the offices, and some offices may lack a customer-service orientation. Customer-relationship management is not a well-understood concept or practice. Students may feel like pawns in a game of 3-D chess trying to navigate the system.

Typically, campuses are structured around academic and service units organized vertically into functional silos. But students are best served horizontally across functional units, because vertical organizational structures do not usually align with needed functions as experienced by students. Another vision, portraying a web of student services, is shown in Figure 2.1 in Chapter Two of this volume. When Web services are created using the old, silo paradigm, students can end up getting the virtual runaround, experiencing many of the same problems and issues that they face in the brick-and-mortar environment. Students may have to log on to multiple systems with multiple IDs and passwords. Every department's Web site may look different, with different navigation buttons located in different locations.

Figure 8.2. Functionality Clusters

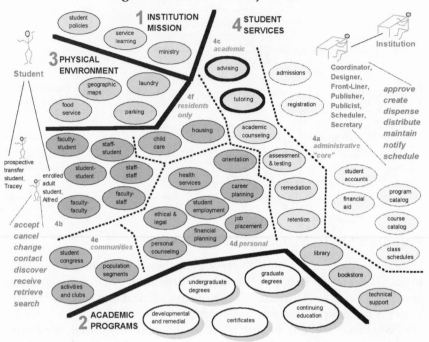

Often the groups creating Web materials don't communicate with one another, and distance education and on-campus Web services aren't linked. A student might be able to initiate part of a process online (order books) but have to complete it (pay for or pick up books) in a face-to-face office. Figure 8.2 provides a visual representation of the Web silo paradigm.

For example, students need to be able to get academic advising (faculty member or advising center), register for classes (registrar's office), pay tuition (business office), get a parking permit (parking office), and purchase textbooks (bookstore) horizontally across functional units—and this even before they have attended a single class! We are moving from a service-based economy to an experience-based economy. The challenge is to provide the student with a positive experience and make the system as easy to navigate as possible. Figure 8.3 shows how services are clustered according to their actual use by students rather than by organizational unit.

Today, in 2005, observers think that many colleges and universities are somewhere between generations two and three in their Web-site development. So, let's assume that you want to move to the next level. How do you do that? How do you move from brochure-ware to a high-tech Web portal with a high-touch experience for your students? How do you use the Web as a tool to help you better manage the relationship between students and your institution?

Figure 8.3. Weaving Silos

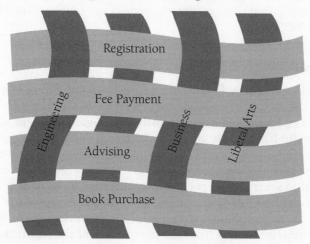

Skill Sets Required to Develop and Manage a Successful Web Site

"Campus Web sites are about community building, and especially the development and nurturing of learning communities" (Kvavik, 1998, p. 1). Developing a successful Web site requires three distinctly different skill sets. It takes excellent technology, superb graphics, and meaningful content to make a Web site successful. The technology must be in place to allow for many university databases to interact with one another to develop dynamic Web sites and make it all happen. The look and feel of the graphics must be easy to navigate and understand and compelling to the end user. The content must speak to and be of relevance to the end user.

The problem is that no one person is likely to have all three needed skill sets to manage even a modest-size Web site successfully—and the size and complexity of most campuses (and campus Web sites) make the task almost impossible! The skill sets required for a high-tech–high-touch Web site cut horizontally across traditional organizational units, with the technology skill sets usually residing in the Information Technology silo, the graphics and branding skill sets usually residing in the Public Affairs silo, and the content knowledge and skills residing in the many, many different academic and service units of the campus.

It should be clear by now that a campus Web site needs to be just that—institution-wide. To truly serve students well, single-unit Web sites or even large, divisional Web sites will not do the job. If the student is to develop a relationship with the Web site (and hence the institution), the site must encompass the entire institution and provide a full range of services.

"The challenge is to make it easy to do business with the organization in any way they want, at any time, through any channel, in any language or currency and to make [constituents] feel that they are dealing with a single, unified organization that recognizes them at any touch point" (Pirani and Salaway, 2005, p.9).

Three Leadership Challenges

Three challenges remain for leaders in student affairs. They are enumerated here.

First Leadership Challenge: Shift Paradigms. Student affairs leaders need to think differently about our Web sites and the roles they can play as critically important parts of our institution. Currently, many on campus think of the Web (if they think of it at all) as a fancy brochure feeding information out to several different constituencies from the multiple perspectives of individual functional units. The Web is organized in a fashion similar to the organizational structure of the university, with content displayed in functional silos from the perspective of the institution. This is first- and second-generation thinking. The paradigm needs to shift to third- and fourth-generation thinking, where the Web is conceived as being a virtual place for developing community and managing customer relationships horizontally across organizational units, with content both sent and received from different constituencies (Conant, 2003). That is, information and interaction are organized and delivered from the perspective of the student (or faculty or staff) customer and is personalized with information about and useful to that person and customized by the person to meet the needs of the community member. The challenge is to provide the end user with an interactive experience that is uniquely theirs. While, ideally, this paradigm shift would occur throughout the university in an instant of recognition of the need, it is far more likely that it will occur incrementally through various units over time.

Organizational paradigm shifting is an area where leadership is truly necessary. There needs to be a champion—or a number of champions—who are willing and able to lead the charge to impart a new vision to decision makers and campus constituents alike to enable them to shift paradigms. Campus leadership needs to recognize which stage their campus Web site is in and agree on which stage they want to move to. The paradigm of the campus Web site as a collection of independent parts needs to shift to a paradigm of the campus Web site as a unified whole that is capable of being individualized for each end user. It is one but also many. The most difficult paradigm shift likely will be to think in terms of an end user or customer focus rather than an institution-centric focus and to conceptualize the Web site working horizontally across functional silos. The Web allows for customer-centric rather than institution-centric processes without having to reorganize staff or relocate brick-and-mortar offices. For example, think about how a student-centric Web site might assist a student who has just been admitted to your institution schedule a face-to-face meeting with her academic adviser, apply for needed financial aid, and find housing on your campus without having to explore several different Web sites. With a student-centric paradigm and proper leadership, we can put the student customer at the center of what we are doing.

Our organizations must learn how to be more flexible, less hierarchical, and broader in functionality. Much of what we do today in terms of our day-to-day operating processes can, should, and will be automated as we move forward. This will free up student affairs professionals to do what they do best—work face-to-face, one-on-one with students, helping them achieve their educational objectives. They will be able to spend far less time on routine matters, which will be handled electronically, and more time dealing directly with students.

Second Leadership Challenge: Develop a Shared Vision for the Web Across the Institution. Critically important is the development of a shared vision for Web-based student services across functional silos and at all levels of the organization. This will not be easy, but if your organization is to have a Web presence that truly encompasses the richness and diversity of the campus, then it is vitally important for there to be a broadly shared vision of what that might look like. The paradigm needs to shift to accommodate the new realities of the twenty-first century. This will require leadership from the president on down to craft such a vision, and there will be resistance to change. These are issues that will have to be overcome. What this means in practical terms will be different on each campus. Each campus will need to develop its own processes to meet this challenge. But speaking generally, the support of the top leadership of the institution is critical. As the division of the university most concerned with student views and issues, student affairs can provide important leadership in helping articulate the students' point of view and in managing student relationships with the university. The chief student affairs officer needs to be able to articulate the vision and help sell it to the president, the vice presidents, the deans, and other top campus leadership. This top-down approach is critical, but so is a bottom-up approach. Departmental directors and front-line staff can be very helpful in articulating the need for change. By working from both top-down and bottom-up approaches, support can be gained across the institution. The broad adoption and acceptance of a vision statement that encompasses fourth-generation concepts is key to success.

Now that you have a new paradigm and a shared vision for what you want in a Web site, you will need to become organized to carry out that vision. In a traditional campus organization, we might be tempted to organize an "Office of Web Management" or some such and establish another silo to manage the Web processes. The problem, of course, is that such a structure rarely works. To manage horizontally—to weave the functional vertical silos of the brick-and-mortar campus into a seamless web—what is needed is a mixed model of cooperation and control—decentralized centralization.

Third Leadership Challenge: Organize to Carry Out the Vision. A key challenge is bringing together a leadership team with the three needed skill sets and the organizational knowledge to organize and manage the web across the functional silos of the university, centralizing what can best be done centrally and decentralizing what can best be done locally. The challenge is to consolidate and yet stay individual by bringing together (virtually or in person) from across the campus the people and tools necessary to do the job. What follows are two recommendations for action.

Develop a cross-functional Web-management leadership team. The team must consist of people with the three distinct and needed skill and knowledge sets and with access to the resources needed to implement the vision. That is, there need to be technological skill sets; graphics, public relations, and branding skill sets; and most important, content knowledge. These three skill sets are needed whether we are talking about a departmental Web site, a divisional Web site, or a university Web site. How one goes about bringing these skills sets together into a functional team will vary at each campus, but often it will be a team of professionals with backgrounds from the Public Affairs and IT areas and subject-matter experts from each functional silo.

Leadership is critical. This team needs to be led by someone who has a broad understanding of the culture, history, business processes, support services, and academic traditions of the institution. While it would be an asset if this person has an understanding and working knowledge of the functional areas, it is not a necessity. This team leader needs to report to someone very high up in the organizational hierarchy so that she or he has the clout necessary to work effectively across the organization.

Identifying people with the needed technology skills and the needed public relations skills should be relatively easy. But how do you get the right people with the content knowledge to serve on the team? There are so many of them spread across the campus that it would be impossible to get them to come together—no less to work together. The answer is that by deploying the right tools (content-management software) you can utilize the skills and talents of many different subject-matter (content) experts from throughout the campus while they work geographically separately but interdependently. This is the decentralized part of our centralization.

Each functional unit that wishes to have a presence on the Web would need to appoint a special Web subject-matter expert to serve in the role of providing and keeping the content for their area accurate and up-to-date through the use of the tools described below. This person would need to know how to use common word processing software but need not have any other special computer skills.

Purchase an appropriate content-management software system. In order to manage the input from the hundreds of subject-matter experts, the institution needs an appropriate content-management software system. Technology tends to amplify organizational habits. Software doesn't magically change human behavior, but without this kind of software, the task of managing Web content quickly becomes overwhelming and the paradigm will not likely change. Most content-management software systems can provide a system that is simple to learn and use and that provides an administrative area for individual department subject-matter experts to manage their unit's content on the campus Web site. These systems can provide a means to manage getting content updated by subject-matter experts (decentralized) while at the same time maintaining a consistent look and feel, maintaining the campus brand, and providing the technological infrastructure to make it all work seamlessly by making use of many campus databases to personalize the Web sites and allow for end-user customization.

Content-management software can be implemented with several different levels. With a quality content-management system, site content can be stored in a database compatible with the campus network environment. The interface to perform updates is completely accessible through any standard Web browser and is easy to learn—no HTML or programming experience required. The simplest level consists of giving each academic department or functional unit the ability to log on to an administrative section through their Web browser. This gives the subject-matter expert access to update all text content of their Web site for immediate posting to the server. The look and feel are managed centrally. A more advanced level of content management brings additional features into the process, such as content approval prior to posting, content expiration notification, the ability to upload and maintain photos and graphics, and more. Like all software, this is a moving target. Several companies are working on this type of software and improving it all the time.

People and tools need to come together so that they can work as a cross-functional team horizontally across functional silos. With the right people with the right skill sets, the right software, and the right technology and infrastructure, meaningful interactive content and services can be delivered to personalized and customized Web sites that uniquely serve the end user (student) with a positive experience that helps promote positive relationships with the campus.

A Call for Leadership

What does this mean for student affairs? Why should student affairs be involved or even consider taking leadership on something like the campus Web? Shouldn't IT or Public Affairs or Academic Affairs take the lead on this one? Student affairs stands at a crossroads. We have the opportunity to take leadership in areas that we already excel in and help move the campus dramatically forward by providing leadership.

We stand at a time of profound change in our society, in our institutions, and in our profession. The real question is how we will meet the challenge of change. Kouzes and Posner (2002) counsel us to have the courage to challenge the process, to search for new opportunities, and to experiment and take risks while we foster collaboration and strengthen others. Covey (2004) tells us that we need to find our own voice first, then help others to find their voices. We are uniquely qualified to help give voice to students and we also have the skill sets and temperament to assist our faculty and staff colleagues.

Student affairs staff have a real opportunity to take a proactive leadership stance and reinvent themselves in the new paradigm of a flat world and a flatter, richly interwoven campus organization. If we do not accept the challenge of leadership, as Chickering has noted, we may be in danger of losing our professional souls: "Challenges to both democracy and higher education are very real. Neither institutions nor individuals claim their souls once and for all; we need serious reflection in these times more than ever if we as an enterprise are to reclaim ours. . . . Reclaiming [our souls] will demand transformations in both our institutions and ourselves as professionals. . . . The major transformation required to reclaim our institutional soul will not be achieved unless our professional souls are similarly respected, supported, and celebrated" (Chickering, 2003, pp. 39, 42–43).

Change has been a hallmark of the student affairs profession. Student affairs has evolved from its roots as an elitist club of anti-intellectual white males "called" to working with college students in the early part of the last century to a broadly diverse group of women and men of all races and backgrounds well educated in a variety of theoretical perspectives with rich and diverse skill sets (Schwartz, 2002). Student affairs professionals know students. Student affairs professionals understand how to build communities. Student affairs professionals understand relationship management as well as or better than most others on campus. Student affairs professionals are specifically qualified in community building and collaboration. The challenge of the Web is to collaborate and innovate.

As Friedman (2005) has made so clear, the world is getting both more complex and, because of technology, "flatter" and easier for all to navigate. Technology has improved the opportunity for many more people from all around the globe to find their own voices and have a place at the table. Much the same is true for our campuses. Technology continues to evolve and improve, bringing about change in our organizations. Technology is helping many organizational structures recognize the need for dramatic change. Geography, whether global or on the campus, becomes largely irrelevant. Our campus organizations, while becoming larger and much more complex to manage in one sense are also becoming easier and easier to navigate because of the impact of technology. If these changes are not breaking down the silo walls, they are at least making them much more permeable. The vertical silo structures that have served us well for many years are being morphed into complex, interwoven structures that serve students both vertically and horizontally across traditional boundaries. Our campuses are starting to be managed by complex, multifunctional teams woven into a tapestry of people, facilitated by technology and collaborating both horizontally and vertically across the campus. This change requires new ways of doing business and new ways of conceptualizing our roles in the academy. The roles of all who serve in the academy are changing—including those in student affairs—perhaps especially those in student affairs.

References

Burnett, D. J. "Innovation in Student Services: Best Practices and Process Innovation Models and Trends." In D. J. Burnett and D. G. Oblinger (eds.), *Innovation in Student Services: Planning for Models Blending High Touch/High Tech.* Ann Arbor: Society for College and University Planning, 2002.

Chaffee, E. "The Complex Future of Higher Education." *Navigator, IV*(II), Spring 2005.

Chickering, A. W. "Reclaiming Our Soul: Democracy and Higher Education." *Change,* Jan./Feb. 2003, pp. 39–44.

Conant, R. "Relationship Management in Higher Education Information Technology." ECAR Research Bulletin, *2003*(13).

Covey, S. R. *The 8th Habit: From Effectiveness to Greatness.* New York: Free Press, 2004.

Friedman, T. L. *The World Is Flat: A Brief History of the Twenty-First Century.* New York: Farrar, Straus & Giroux, 2005.

Gottesman, B. Z. "Microsoft's Vision," *PC Magazine,* Sept. 2000, p. 84.

Kouzes, J. M., and Posner, B. Z. *The Leadership Challenge* (3rd ed.). San Francisco: Jossey-Bass, 2002.

Krotz, J. L. "What Kind of Web Site Does Your Business Need?" http://www.microsoft.com/smallbusiness/issues/marketing/online_marketing/what_kind_of_Web_site_does_your_business_need.mspx. Accessed May 2005.

Kvavik, R. B. "Transforming Student Services." Paper presented at Innovations in Student Services Forum, Brigham Young University, August 1998.

Pirani, J. A., and Salaway, G. *IT Networking in Higher Education.* Denver, Colo.: EDUCAUSE Center for Applied Research, 2005.

Schwartz, R. A. "The Rise and Demise of Deans of Men." *The Review of Higher Education,* Winter 2002, *26*(2), 217–239.

Wager, J. J. "Support Services for the Net Generation." In D. G. Oblinger and J. L. Oblinger (eds.), *Educating the Net Generation.* http://www.educause.edu/educatingthenetgen. Accessed May 2005.

GARY L. KLEEMANN is director of e-learning at Arizona State University East.

9

In this summary chapter, the author presents a series of key issues that should be addressed by student affairs professionals in their planning and work with students.

What We Know and the Difference It Makes

Kevin Kruger

If you have read the previous eight chapters, you have a solid overview of the issues and opportunities related to the use of technology in student affairs. There are several themes that benefit from review and summary. The current capabilities of technology now and in the next several years provide unprecedented opportunities to improve the learning experience of our students, and student affairs should be in the best position to take advantage of these opportunities.

In 2005, as this chapter is written, the use of technology by college students has been well documented. A quick review reveals a student population fully engaged in information technology:

Recent surveys suggest that more than 85 percent of students go online daily, spending more than twelve hours per week online (Student Monitor, 2004).

While online, more than 80 percent of students access their e-mail and use instant messaging (IM) daily. The most frequently accessed Web sites are music related, where student browse, listen, and download music files (both legally and illegally).

A full 65 percent of students surveyed report being regular game players, using PC-based games, console games (X-Box, Playstation), or online games (Jones, 2003).

Interestingly, despite common stereotypes, 60 percent of online game players among college students are women (Jones, 2003).

New Directions for Student Services, no. 112, Winter 2005 © Wiley Periodicals, Inc.

Close to half of college-student gamers agreed that gaming keeps them from studying (Jones, 2003).

In addition, 9 percent of students admitted that their main motivation for playing games was to avoid studying (Jones, 2003).

And in one of the most challenging statistics, one-third of students surveyed admitted playing games during class that were not part of instructional activities (Jones, 2003).

The results of the "Health Survey" conducted by the American College Health Association found that more than 14 percent of students who report a serious academic consequence (dropped class, poor grade, incomplete coursework) cite time spent on the Internet and computer gaming as a cause (ACHA, 2004).

For our students who make up the "Net Generation" (Tapscott, 1998), what we consider as technology comprises the most basic aspects of their environment. "For Net-Geners, technologies that are still considered transformative by their parents' and grandparents' standards (for example, instant messaging) are a basic part of their everyday lives; they are only considering technology in the broadest sense of the term. . . . For the Net Generation, technology is 'what's new' and the time between new and old can be quite brief when viewed from a perspective other than the Net Generation's" (Roberts, 2005, p. 3.2). What this suggests is that as student affairs leaders, we cannot chase the technology—meaning that we can be neither influenced nor seduced by the lure of the latest technology and how to implement this technology into our practice simply because students are using the technology. Instead of the technology driving the innovation, we need to have more conversations about creating the best learning environments and the ways in which technology can enhance those environments.

In addition to the futility of chasing the newest technologies, it is sobering to examine the challenges to implementing basic technologies. A good example is the implementation of electronic portfolios on campus. Bresciani described in Chapter Six the tremendous potential of electronic portfolios in assessment and student learning. Electronic portfolios also have great potential in developing co-curricular transcripts as well as providing an evidence-based tool for service learning and for documenting out-of-class competencies for career development purposes. Despite the inherent value of portfolios in student and academic affairs, only 24 percent of public research and 5 percent of community colleges report active portfolio projects (Green, 2003). Why? As reported by NACUBO (National Association of College and University Business Officers) and EDUCAUSE, "Total costs for IT are increasing at a rate that exceeds higher education's ability to pay" (EDUCAUSE, 2003, p. 1). Budget cuts in higher education, heavy investments in technology infrastructure, the pace of new technologies, and new security requirements all create a challenging environment to implement even the most obviously beneficial technologies.

Focus on the Student

Students' use and reliance on technology presents both opportunities and challenges to our work as student affairs professionals. What follows are a range of key issues and questions that should be a part of the dialogue with staff in long-range conversations about technology.

Students have been raised with computers. As a result, they deal with information in a different way. They are more likely to leap around when seeking information, they jump from task to task, they think in hypertext rather than in a linear way (Oblinger, 2005). Having become accustomed to having multiple windows open on their computer, they are equally comfortable multitasking in the other parts of their world. What are the implications of this kind of learning and thinking? What does this mean for our programs and the ways we teach?

Through orientation, advising, and other interactions with students, we need to help develop their ability to distinguish what information acquired through the Internet is trustworthy. The Educational Testing Service, for example, has developed a test that will measure "Internet Intelligence." The test has been designed to assess students' "abilities to locate information, choose appropriate sources from search results, and properly cite the sources of information they would use for a project" (San Jose Mercury News, 2005, p. 1B). The needs of students to function as scholars in the academic community suggest important opportunities for student affairs professionals to partner with faculty in teaching Internet skills to new students.

Recognizing the significant amounts of time students spend on technology, student affairs professionals would be well served to inquire about time spent gaming, instant messaging, Internet gambling, and in online chat in their interactions with students. Negative consequences, including Internet addiction, should be identified as a potential issue with frontline staff. "Substitute the word 'computer' for 'substance' or 'alcohol' and you find that Internet obsession fits the classic *Diagnostic [and] Statistical Manual* definition of addiction" (Murray, 2005). Does your counseling center program offer groups or interventions in Internet addiction? Have your frontline staff, particularly live-in staff, been trained to identify symptoms of Internet addiction and referral options? In an article called "Getting Caught in the Net," Kendall, a counselor at the University of Maryland, suggests that students take a series of steps to address Internet addiction:

- Break the pattern of Internet use
- Find something else to do when you first get home rather than using the computer
- Set an alarm clock to force you offline after an hour

- Find other uses for time
- Find other people and talk
- Examine the underlying issues for the amount of time you are spending online (Kendall, 2000).

Technology provides rich opportunities to connect to students in meaningful ways. In addition, the community-building and relationship-building features of technology need to be explored more fully to take advantage of the time students are spending online. Instant messaging, chat rooms, and discussion boards all provide opportunities to interact with students. In this way, the experience of faculty who have been teaching online courses is instructive to our own work with students outside of the classroom. "As a community, we've learned that while e-mail and discussion boards aren't the same as the live classroom, they have their own unique instructional effectiveness. And, indeed, for some interactions and purposes, the online space actually is better. The shy students seem to talk more; students often graciously engage and support each other; they seem to reflect and express more thoughtful ideas in online forums; and busy students can learn anytime, anywhere" (Boettcher, 2005). The power of these online interactions suggests looking at untapped communication opportunities and the way student affairs professionals might interact with students.

In Chapter Four, Dare, Zapata, and Thomas discuss research on the needs of the distance learner. It is often common, however, for campuses that offer distance learning courses to discover that a significant percentage of students enrolled in distance courses are campus-based students. In addition, Dare's research suggests that distance learners have needs and interests in many of the student services, support services, and community-building programs and activities that are made available to campus-based students. Student affairs departments need to be more involved in the movement to create online student services for distance learners. Rather than look at campus-based students and distance learners as two completely separate populations, traditional student affairs functions will need to expand their programs to meet the needs of this ever-increasing student population.

This volume has sought to create the opportunity for new dialogues within staff meetings, strategic planning sessions, or departmental planning sessions. The effect of technology on student affairs work is immense. It has transformed the higher education experience and is transforming the work of student affairs professionals. It is my hope that these authors have added to the important dialogue regarding the role technology will play in the evolution of the student affairs profession.

References

American College Health Association (ACHA). "National College Health Assessment, Fall 2004." http://www.acha.org/projects_programs/IMPEDIMENTSF04.cfm. Accessed May 1, 2005.

Boettcher, J. V. "Designing for the Virtual Interactive Classroom." *Campus Technology,* May 2005. http://www.campus-technology.com/article.asp?id=11046. Accessed May 1, 2005.

EDUCAUSE. *Funding Information Technology: An EDUCAUSE Executive Briefing.* 2003. http://www.educause.edu/ir/library/pdf/pub4002.pdf. Accessed May 1, 2005.

Green, K. C. "Tracking the Digital Puck into 2004." *Syllabus,* Dec. 1, 2003. http://www.campus-technology.com/article.asp?id=8574. Accessed May 1, 2005.

Jones, S. "Let the Games Begin: Gaming Technology and Entertainment Among College Students." Pew Internet & American Life Project, July 6, 2003. http://www.pewinternet.org/PPF/r/93/report_display.asp. Accessed May 1, 2005.

Kendall, J. "Getting Caught in the Net." http://www.inform.umd.edu/CampusInfo/Departments/Counseling/selfhelp/sh_ne/tad.htm. Accessed May 1, 2005.

Murray, B. "Computer Addictions Entangle Students." Center for Online Addiction. http://www.healthyplace.com/Communities/Addictions/netaddiction/articles/apa_computer_addictions_students.htm. Accessed May 31, 2005.

Oblinger, D. G. "Is it Age or IT? First Steps Toward Understanding the Net Generation." In D. G. Oblinger and J. L. Oblinger (eds.), *Educating the Net Generation.* 2005. http://www.educause.edu/educatingthenetgen. Accessed May 31, 2005.

Roberts, G. "Technology and Learning Expectations of the Net Generation." In D. G. Oblinger and J. L. Oblinger (eds.), *Educating the Net Generation.* 2005. http://www.educause.edu/educatingthenetgen. Accessed May 31, 2005.

Student Monitor. *Lifestyle and Media Study.* Ridgewood, N.J.: Student Monitor, Spring 2004. http://www.studentmonitor.com. Accessed May 1, 2005.

Tapscott, D. *Growing Up Digital.* New York: McGraw-Hill, 1998.

"Testing the Smarts of Today's Students." *San Jose Mercury News,* July 1, 2005.

KEVIN KRUGER *is associate executive director of the National Association of Student Personnel Administrators (NASPA).*

INDEX

Back Issue/Subscription Order Form

Copy or detach and send to:
Jossey-Bass, A Wiley Imprint, 989 Market Street, San Francisco CA, 94103-1741

Call or fax toll-free: Phone 888-378-2537 6:30AM – 3PM PST; Fax 888-481-2665

Back Issues: Please send me the following issues at $27 each
(Important: please include ISBN number for each issue.)

_____

_____

_____

$ _____   Total for single issues

$ _____   SHIPPING CHARGES: SURFACE   Domestic Canadian
                                      First Item $5.00 $6.00
                                      Each Add'l Item $3.00 $1.50
                      For next-day and second-day delivery rates, call the number listed above.

Subscriptions   Please __ start __ renew my subscription to *New Directions for Student
                Services* for the year 2_____at the following rate:

U.S.	__ Individual $75	__ Institutional $180
Canada	__ Individual $75	__ Institutional $220
All Others	__ Individual $99	__ Institutional $254

**For more information about online subscriptions visit
www.wileyinterscience.com**

$ Total single issues and subscriptions (Add appropriate sales tax
              for your state for single issue orders. No sales tax for U.S.
_____ subscriptions. Canadian residents, add GST for subscriptions and
              single issues.)

__Payment enclosed (U.S. check or money order only)

__VISA __ MC __ AmEx Card #_____Exp.Date_____

Signature _____ Day Phone _____

__Bill Me (U.S. institutional orders only. Purchase order required.)

Purchase order # _____
                 Federal Tax ID13559302   **GST 89102 8052**

Name_____

Address_____

_____

Phone_____ E-mail_____

For more information about Jossey-Bass, visit our Web site at www.josseybass.com

**NEW DIRECTIONS FOR STUDENT SERVICES
IS NOW AVAILABLE ONLINE AT WILEY INTERSCIENCE**

What is Wiley InterScience?

Wiley InterScience is the dynamic online content service from John Wiley &
Sons delivering the full text of over 300 leading scientific, technical, medical,
and professional journals, plus major reference works, the acclaimed *Current
Protocols* laboratory manuals, and even the full text of select Wiley print books
online.

What are some special features of Wiley InterScience?

Wiley InterScience Alerts is a service that delivers table of contents via e-mail
for any journal available on Wiley InterScience as soon as a new issue is
published online.
Early View is Wiley's exclusive service presenting individual articles online as
soon as they are ready, even before the release of the compiled print issue.
These articles are complete, peer-reviewed, and citable.
CrossRef is the innovative multi-publisher reference linking system enabling
readers to move seamlessly from a reference in a journal article to the cited
publication, typically located on a different server and published by a different
publisher.

How can I access Wiley InterScience?

Visit http://www.interscience.wiley.com

Guest Users can browse Wiley InterScience for unrestricted access to journal
Tables of Contents and Article Abstracts, or use the powerful search engine.
Registered Users are provided with a *Personal Home Page* to store and
manage customized alerts, searches, and links to favorite journals and articles.
Additionally, Registered Users can view free Online Sample Issues and preview
selected material from major reference works.
Licensed Customers are entitled to access full-text journal articles in PDF, with
select journals also offering full-text HTML.

How do I become an Authorized User?

Authorized Users are individuals authorized by a paying Customer to have
access to the journals in Wiley InterScience. For example, a university that
subscribes to Wiley journals is considered to be the Customer. Faculty, staff and
students authorized by the university to have access to those journals in Wiley
InterScience are Authorized Users. Users should contact their Library for information on which Wiley journals they have access to in Wiley InterScience.

ASK YOUR INSTITUTION ABOUT WILEY INTERSCIENCE TODAY!

United States Postal Service
Statement of Ownership, Management, and Circulation

1. Publication Title	2. Publication Number									3. Filing Date
New Directions For Student Services	0	1	6	4	–	7	9	7	0	10/1/05

4. Issue Frequency	5. Number of Issues Published Annually	6. Annual Subscription Price
Quarterly	4	$180.00

7. Complete Mailing Address of Known Office of Publication *(Not printer) (Street, city, county, state, and ZIP+4)*

Wiley Subscription Services, Inc. at Jossey-Bass, 989 Market Street, San Francisco, CA 94103

Contact Person
Joe Schuman
Telephone
(415) 782-3232

8. Complete Mailing Address of Headquarters or General Business Office of Publisher *(Not printer)*

Wiley Subscription Services, Inc. 111 River Street, Hoboken, NJ 07030

9. Full Names and Complete Mailing Addresses of Publisher, Editor, and Managing Editor *(Do not leave blank)*

Publisher *(Name and complete mailing address)*

Wiley, San Francisco, 989 Market Street, San Francisco, CA 94103-1741

Editor *(Name and complete mailing address)*

John H. Schuh, N243 Lagomarcino Hall, Iowa State University, Ames, IA 50011

Managing Editor *(Name and complete mailing address)*

None

10. Owner *(Do not leave blank. If the publication is owned by a corporation, give the name and address of the corporation immediately followed by the names and addresses of all stockholders owning or holding 1 percent or more of the total amount of stock. If not owned by a corporation, give the names and addresses of the individual owners. If owned by a partnership or other unincorporated firm, give its name and address as well as those of each individual owner. If the publication is published by a nonprofit organization, give its name and address.)*

Full Name	Complete Mailing Address
Wiley Subscription Services, Inc.	111 River Street, Hoboken, NJ 07030
(see attached list)	

11. Known Bondholders, Mortgagees, and Other Security Holders Owning or Holding 1 Percent or More of Total Amount of Bonds, Mortgages, or Other Securities. If none, check box. ☑ None

Full Name	Complete Mailing Address
None	None

12. Tax Status *(For completion by nonprofit organizations authorized to mail at nonprofit rates) (Check one)*
The purpose, function, and nonprofit status of this organization and the exempt status for federal income tax purposes:
☐ Has Not Changed During Preceding 12 Months
☐ Has Changed During Preceding 12 Months *(Publisher must submit explanation of change with this statement)*

PS Form 3526, October 1999   *(See Instructions on Reverse)*

---

13. Publication Title	14. Issue Date for Circulation Data Below
New Directions For Student Services	Summer 2005

15.	Extent and Nature of Circulation		Average No. Copies Each Issue During Preceding 12 Months	No. Copies of Single Issue Published Nearest to Filing Date
a.	Total Number of Copies *(Net press run)*		1591	1563
b. Paid and/or Requested Circulation	(1)	Paid/Requested Outside-County Mail Subscriptions Stated on Form 3541. *(Include advertiser's proof and exchange copies)*	536	494
	(2)	Paid In-County Subscriptions Stated on Form 3541 *(Include advertiser's proof and exchange copies)*	0	0
	(3)	Sales Through Dealers and Carriers, Street Vendors, Counter Sales, and Other Non-USPS Paid Distribution	0	0
	(4)	Other Classes Mailed Through the USPS	0	0
c.	Total Paid and/or Requested Circulation *[Sum of 15b. (1), (2),(3),and (4)]* ▶		536	494
d. Free Distribution by Mail *(Samples, complimentary, and other free)*	(1)	Outside-County as Stated on Form 3541	0	0
	(2)	In-County as Stated on Form 3541	0	0
	(3)	Other Classes Mailed Through the USPS	0	0
e.	Free Distribution Outside the Mail *(Carriers or other means)*		89	90
f.	Total Free Distribution *(Sum of 15d. and 15e.)* ▶		89	90
g.	Total Distribution *(Sum of 15c. and 15f)* ▶		625	584
h.	Copies not Distributed		966	979
i.	Total *(Sum of 15g. and h.)* ▶		1591	1563
j.	Percent Paid and/or Requested Circulation *(15c. divided by 15g. times 100)*		86%	85%

16. Publication of Statement of Ownership
☑ Publication required. Will be printed in the __Winter 2005__ issue of this publication. ☐ Publication not required.

17. Signature and Title of Editor, Publisher, Business Manager, or Owner

Susan E. Lewis, VP & Publisher - Periodicals

Date
10/01/05

I certify that all information furnished on this form is true and complete. I understand that anyone who furnishes false or misleading information on this form or who omits material or information requested on the form may be subject to criminal sanctions (including fines and imprisonment) and/or civil sanctions (including civil penalties).

Instructions to Publishers

1. Complete and file one copy of this form with your postmaster annually on or before October 1. Keep a copy of the completed form for your records.

2. In cases where the stockholder or security holder is a trustee, include in items 10 and 11 the name of the person or corporation for whom the trustee is acting. Also include the names and addresses of individuals who are stockholders who own or hold 1 percent or more of the total amount of bonds, mortgages, or other securities of the publishing corporation. In item 11, if none, check the box. Use blank sheets if more space is required.

3. Be sure to furnish all circulation information called for in item 15. Free circulation must be shown in items 15d, e, and f.

4. Item 15h., Copies not Distributed, must include (1) newsstand copies originally stated on Form 3541, and returned to the publisher, (2) estimated returns from news agents, and (3), copies for office use, leftovers, spoiled, and all other copies not distributed.

5. If the publication had Periodicals authorization as a general or requester publication, this Statement of Ownership, Management, and Circulation must be published; it must be printed in any issue in October or, if the publication is not published during October, the first issue printed after October.

6. In item 16, indicate the date of the issue in which this Statement of Ownership will be published.

7. Item 17 must be signed.

Failure to file or publish a statement of ownership may lead to suspension of Periodicals authorization.

PS Form 3526, October 1999 *(Reverse)*